Gisburn Church

THE OLD PARISH CHURCHES
OF LANCASHIRE
Mike Salter

FOLLY PUBLICATIONS

ACKNOWLEDGEMENTS

The photographs and measured drawings in this book are mostly the product of the author's fieldwork between 1977 and 2005. Old postcards and brass rubbings are reproduced from originals in the author's collection. Thanks are due to Max Barfield and Helen Thomas for help with transport on fieldtrips. Paul Adkins helped solve computer problems, and Allan and Paul of Aspect Design put the book together ready for printing.

ABOUT THIS BOOK

As with the other books in this series (see full list on the inside of the back cover) this book concentrates on the period before the Industrial Revolution of the late 18th century. Most furnishings and monuments after 1800 are not mentioned, but additions and alterations to the fabric usually are, although in less detail. The numerous churches founded after 1800 to serve the new urban areas do not appear in the gazetteer, or on the map.

For the purposes of this book Lancashire is treated as though it still includes the districts of Manchester and Liverpool. The book includes several churches formerly in a part of the West Riding of Yorkshire which became part of Lancashire at the 1974 boundary changes. Lancashire north of the sands became part of Cumbria in 1974 and old churches in that district have already been described in the companion volume for Cumbria.

The book is inevitably very much a catalogue of dates and names, etc. It is intended as a field guide and for reference rather than to be read straight from cover to cover. Occasionally there is a comment about the setting of a church but on the whole little is said about their location or atmosphere. Also, notable features of one or two buildings may lay outside the scope of this book. Visit them and judge for yourself. The book is intended to be used in conjunction with the O.S. 1:50,000 scale maps, and a six-figure grid reference appears after each place-name and dedication.

Plans redrawn from originals in the author's collection are reproduced to a common scale of 1:400. The buildings were measured in metres and only metric scales are given. A hatching system common to all the plans is used to denote the different periods of work. The plans should be treated with care and cross-referenced with the text since there are some things difficult to convey on small-scale drawings (eg stones on one period being reset or reused in a later period). In some cases walling is shown on a plan as being of a specific century when it is in fact very difficult to date with any accuracy.

ABOUT THE AUTHOR

Mike Salter is 52 and has been a professional author and publisher since 1988. He is particularly interested in the planning and layout of medieval buildings and has a huge collection of plans of castles and churches he has measured during tours (mostly by bicycle and motorcycle) throughout all parts of the British Isles since 1968. Wolverhampton born and bred, Mike now lives in an old cottage beside the Malvern Hills. His other interests include walking, maps, railways, board games, morris dancing and playing percussion instruments and calling folk dances with an occasional folk group.

IBSN 1 871731 69 0

First published December 2005. Copyright 2005 Mike Salter
Folly Publications, Folly Cottage, 151 West Malvern Rd, Malvern, Worcs, WR14 4AY
Printed by Aspect Design, 89 Newtown Rd, Malvern, Worcestershire, WR14 2PD

This book is dedicated to the men and women of Old Meg, a Malvern based morris team which has performed dances from several of the places mentioned in this book.

Bracewell Church

CONTENTS

INTRODUCTION

Not much is known about the early history of Christianity in Lancashire. Throughout the medieval period the county was divided at the Ribble into two archdeaconries. The northern part was included in the archdiocese of York, an arrangement which lasted from the Saxon period until a new diocese of Blackburn was created in 1926. Churches south of the Ribble came under the bishopric of Lichfield until a new bishopric was established at Chester in 1541. This part is now divided between more recent bishoprics of Manchester and Liverpool established in 1847 and 1880 respectively. Ecclesiastical remains earlier than the period of the Domesday Book land survey of 1086 carried out on the orders of William I are limited to fragments of crosses or monuments at a dozen places, some walling at Lancaster, and two buildings each preserving a Saxon doorway at Heysham, where there is also a hogback gravestone. The smaller of the buildings at Heysham is a chapel of St Patrick going back to the 8th or 9th century. Most of the cross fragments are 10th or 11th century. The cross at Winwick appears to have been large.

Medieval churches were never as numerous in Lancashire as in many other English counties and of the 136 churches described in this book only just over half have actual standing remains dating before the Reformation of the 1530s and 40s. Less than fifty are essentially medieval structures as they now stand. In the medieval period Lancashire was fairly sparsely populated, much of it being wooded, and there seem to have only been about 56 churches by the 1290s, when there is a record of 48 of them being taxed by Pope Nicholas. At the time of Domesday Book there may only have been about two dozen large parishes in Lancashire, each with a single mother church, but chapels-of-ease were eventually erected in a number of places and in time many of these became parish churches in their own right. Lancashire has an unusually high proportion of churches dating from the period between the Reformation and the Industrial Revolution, whilst the majority of Anglican churches in the area covered by this book are in fact 19th century structures lying outside the scope of the book.

St Patrick's Chapel, Heysham

Norman doorway at Gressingham   *Norman doorway at Aughton*

About thirty churches have some relic of a 12th century Norman building but the chapel at Stydd and the church at Bracewell are the only buildings of this period remaining anything like complete, and both these are much altered. Doorways remain at Aughton, Gressingham, Overton, Tatham and Whalley, but other remains are limited to small bits of walling, a font, or just a few carved stones either reset or lying loose. Most churches in this period had two chambers, each dimly lighted by small round-headed windows. The chancel contained the altar and its attendant priest whilst the much larger nave with round-headed doorways usually on both the north and south sides contained the congregation, most of whom at this period would have stood throughout the duration of a service. At Overton and Lancaster foundations have been revealed of a semi-circular apse at the east end. In England apses went out of fashion after the 1170s, and were usually eventually replaced by larger square-ended chancels containing enough space for a choir as well as the altar and priest, but there is an early 16th century apse at Hornby.

Only about twenty churches contain 13th century work. Ribchester and Whalley have a fine chancels with priest's doorways and several of the slender pointed-headed lancet windows then in vogue, and Whalley has a complete aisled nave also, but most of the work is no more than bits of walling, or a doorway as at Stydd. As congregations grew the churches were enlarged, often by added a lean-to roofed aisle on one side, or both. There is no certain evidence that any Lancashire parish church possessed an aisle earlier than c1200, the date of the arcade opening into the north aisle at Colne. Arcades of pointed arches set upon octagonal piers remain of 13th century aisles at Kirkland and Rochdale. St Michaels on Wyre and Tunstall had both north and south aisles in the 13th century, and Bolton-by-Bowland had at least a south aisle. In all these instances the aisles themselves have suffered rebuilding, often being increased in width either in the later medieval or Victorian periods. In some cases the west windows of the early aisles still survive but larger new windows have been provided later in the side walls.

Late-Saxon cross at Whalley

Nearly thirty Lancashire churches have work of the period 1300-1400. Great Mitton has a nave and chancel of c1300 with windows with Y-tracery, a development from placing two lancets together and piercing the space between the heads. Windows at Kirkland show the next development, having more lights and with the lights cusped. These windows are part of the architectural style usually known as Decorated. What is now a nave at Upholland was intended to be the aisled chancel of a monastic church. A north aisle at Ribchester has a very unusual pier with a tri-lobed section. Other remains are mostly of much altered aisles or chancels, but several towers date from this period, notable examples being at Sefton and Winwick. The tower at Aughton is placed in a north transeptal position, a similar tower at Ormskirk lies at the west end of the south aisle, and Warrington has a central tower (entirely renewed in later periods) but the most common location for a tower is at the west end of the nave. The only earlier towers are those probably of 12th century date at the churches of Bracewell and Gisburn, both in the Bowland district formerly in the West Riding of Yorkshire.

Over Kellet Church

Most of the medieval work remaining in the churches of Lancashire is in the Perpendicular style introduced in the late 14th century, the probable date of the eastern parts of Lancaster Priory church. This style remained in vogue for almost two centuries but as the 16th century wore on windows tended to have little or no tracery and cusping was discontinued in the heads of the lights. Much of the work was executed in the period 1480-1530 and cannot be precisely assigned to one century or another, but about twenty towers appear to be 15th century and another fifteen towers are considered to be 16th century work. A tower of c1400 at Halsall with an octagonal top stage and spire has pairs of corner buttresses, and the 15th century towers at Colne, Burnley, Manchester, Prestwich, Slaidburn, Waddington, Walton-le-Dale and Whalley are similarly buttressed. The other towers have diagonal buttresses. Ormskirk has a huge mid 16th century tower 12m square in addition to the adjacent late 14th century tower. Most of these towers have a spiral staircase contained in a square turret set at either the NE or SE corner. They are generally embattled and without spires. Hornby is a quite exceptional case, having an early 16th century west tower which is octagonal throughout its height, in addition to an unusual apsed east end of the same period.

The church at Manchester was rebuilt after being made collegiate in the early 15th century and eventually had a fully aisled nave and chancel with numerous outer chapels effectively forming outer aisles. Most of the existing stonework, however, is no older than the 19th century, although it mostly reproduces the church as it stood c1500 with large windows of four lights separated only by buttresses. Extra light for the nave and chancel was obtained by rows of clerestory windows over the arcades. They ocurred at earlier periods but surviving pre-Victorian clerestories in Lancashire are 15th, 16th or 17th century in date. Churches such as Bolton-by-Bowland, Deane, Gisburn, Goosenargh, St Michael's-on-Wyre, Samlesbury, Sefton, Tunstall, and Winwick all appear to be essentially late medieval (here meaning c1400-1560) externally, although all of them contain significant older parts. Like many North country churches they mostly appear as long and low embattled buildings with chancels the same height as the naves and square-headed side windows of moderate height. Lydiate is an unaltered but badly ruined late 15th century chantry chapel. Altham has a modest 16th century church with an aisled nave, although the tower and chancel have been rebuilt. Standish has a fine fully aisled 16th century church where only the tower and vestries are later. Here parts of the east end may be as late as the 1580s. Most churches had been provided with at least one porch by the late 16th century, the south doorway usually being so favoured except for where the approach to the building was from the north. Some of the greater churches have a 15th or 16th century vestry, always located on the north side of the chancel towards the east end, as at Kirkland.

13th century doorway capitals at Stydd

Overton Church.

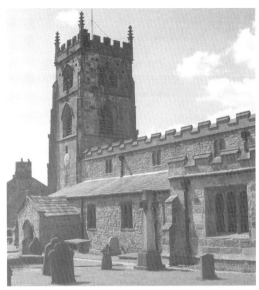

Bolton-by-Bowland Church   *Timber-framed church at Denton*

Denton has a rare example of a 16th century timber-framed church although very little of the existing structure is now ancient. At one time there were probably several other churc es in southern Lancashire that were partly or wholly timber-framed, and it is likely that many of the pre-Norman churches took this form. Rivington has another rarity, a small detached bell-house probably of c1600.

The 17th century was a period when in most counties there was little building work going on in churches apart from minor repairs and the occasional addition of a tower, chapel or porch, although furnishings are usually numerous. In Lancashire there are a few towers, all of minor importance, and in several cases older towers were rebuilt or replaced, as at Didsbury, where the aisled nave is also 17th century, and Warrington, where the central tower now dates from the 1690s. Prescot has arcades of this period, along with the nave roof, whilst Hoole has a small brick church of 1628.

Lancashire is unusually rich in 18th century churches, having about thirty which are essentially of that period, although some were altered or extended later on. The majority were new foundations, quite a lot of them the result of growth of urban areas necessitating new churches in the suburbs, a trend which continued at an even faster rate during the 19th century. St Anne's in Manchester was built in 1709-12, there are churches of c1750-60 at Lancaster, Poulton-le-Fylde and Salford, and others of the 1780s and 90s at Blackburn and Liverpool. Of brick with stone dressings are a church of 1740 at Rochdale and others of the 1780s and 90s at Bolton and Wigan. These are all classical style buildings with columns supporting galleries on each side, and most of them have a west tower. Other churches of this period in rural locations are smaller and more rustic, not all of them having towers. Hale is an instance of an 18th century church with a Venetian east window and a medieval west tower. Wood Plumpton is a hybrid, having arched windows with keystones, but also an embattled parapet, although there also genuine medieval parts surviving there. Of other additions to older churches the large west tower at Prescot needs to be mentioned.

Old tower at Ringley

Becconsall Church

During the 19th century all of the older churches were restored. In many cases this amounted to almost an entire rebuilding, towers being the most likely part to escape such treatment. Many of the churches of southern Lancashire were built of soft sandstones which soon show signs of wear, and the polluted air caused by industrialisation did not help. Even most of the 18th century churches suffered some remodelling, additions which changed their character outside, or refurbishment inside. Many ancient furnishings and funerary monuments were lost or damaged during these works and what now remains is only a small fraction of what once existed

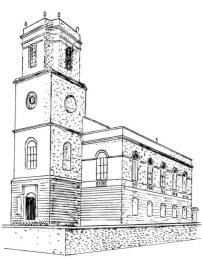

Holy Trinity Church, Liverpool

Bell-house at Rivington

Font at Preston

A few churches still have medieval fonts and there are several of the 1660s, suggesting that many were removed during the Civil War period because of symbols upon them which the Puritans objected to. One dated 1663 at Croston has quatrefoils, another dated 1661 at Ormskirk has several motifs and Charles II's initials. A Norman font at Kirkby has roll-mouldings and figures of seven saints, and another at Huyton has heads in arcading and a rosette frieze. Later medieval fonts are usually octagonal with various combinations of quatrefoils, carved heads and shields, as at Colne and Preston, whilst that at Waddington has shields bearing the Instruments of the Passion. Several 18th century fonts are baluster-shaped, as at Denton, Lowton, and Wigan. Fonts were sometimes fitted with covers, one such at Great Mitton being dated 1593, and another at Sefton is dated 1688

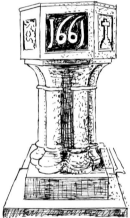

Font at Ormskirk

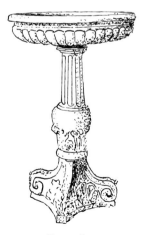

Font at Prescot

Heapey Church

Tower at Garstang

It was the custom for the chancels of churches to be divided off from the nave by a screen to emphasise the greater sanctity of the east end. The screen dividing off the chancel became known as the Rood screen from the Holy Rood or image of the crucifixion often mounted upon it. Sometimes there was a loft over the screen for the use of musicians and the performers of religious plays. Many rood screens and their lofts were ripped out by Puritan reformers in the late 16th and 17th centuries, and others were removed or cut down to the dado (the solid lower part) during 19th century restorations. Stairs beside an arcade pier or within the outer wall which gave access to the loft sometimes remain as a reminder of a long-lost screen and loft. Lancashire was a conservative county and there was still considerable support for Catholicism far beyond the Reformation of the 1530s and 40s. This may explain the rood-loft staircases at Standish, which are probably no earlier than the 1550s. The screens at Sefton are also likely to be of the 1530s or 40s A fine screen of c1500 at Huyton was removed in the 1640s to protect it from being destroyed and replaced after the Restoration of Charles II in 1660. Other notable screens of the late medieval period survive at Manchester, Middleton, Northenden, and Rochdale. There are also fine wrought-iron screens of the mid 18th century in Manchester Cathedral.

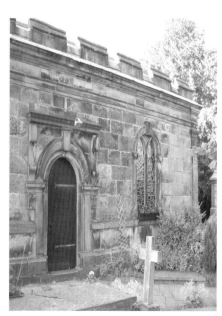

Wood Plumpton Church

Monument at Great Mitton

*Stall canopies at
Lancaster Priory*

Stalls at Prescot

Medieval pulpits rarely survive in English churches. In any case it was only after the Reformation that long sermons became an important part of services. Several pulpits which look Elizabethan are in fact early or mid 17th century, as at Ribchester and Standish. Pulpits of the 17th and 18th centuries remain in quite a number of churches, those at Barnoldswick, Pilling and Slaidburn being of the three decker type with desks at lower levels for lay readers. Samlesbury has a two-decker pulpit. Old pews tend to take two forms, the late medieval bench type with tall ends often carved with poppyheads and sometimes bearing initials, arms or dates as at Halsall, Old Langho, and Sefton, and the box-pew type favoured from the late 17th century until the mid 19th century, as at Barnoldswick. Chorley has a pair of ornate family pews of the 17th century. Several churches have 18th century chandeliers, Lancaster Priory church having a set of three. Medieval doors are a rarity but occasionally older ironwork was transplanted onto a newer door. Some churches have 17th and 18th century altar rails. The set at Upholland with twisted balusters is fairly typical. Plate was kept in chests and these occasionally survive. Stalls with miserichords or hinged seats survive in the churches of Blackburn, Bolton, Halsall, Lancaster Priory, Manchester, Middleton and Whalley. Those at Lancaster and Manchester remain in situ with fine canopies above them. Of the fine sets of stained glass windows that many of the churches must have once possessed all that remains are a few minor fragments at Ashton-under-Lyne, Eccleston, Gisburn, Middleton, St Michael's-on-Wyre, Samlesbury and Upholland. Little remains of the wall-paintings which would have adorned most of the walls of all medieval churches. An Ascension scene remains at St Michael's-on-Wyre.

Miserichord seat at Whalley

Royal Arms at Over Kellet

Pulpit at Standish

Hatchments at Bolton-by-Bowland

Effigy at Standish

The best surviving medieval monumental effigies in Lancashire take the form of engraved brasses. Of the period c1450-1530 are a knight at Ormskirk, a college warden, a bishop and a couple at Manchester, a priest at Eccleston, two knights at Winwick, and a man and wife at Childwall. Middleton has a collection of smaller brasses of the 16th and 17th centuries, and there are others at Bolton-by-Bowland and Whalley with early 16th century figures depicted kneeling in prayer. Bolton-by-Bowland has a tombchest with rows of figures in half-relief on the lid, and there are alabaster slabs with figures outlined in engraved lines inlaid with pitch at Radcliffe, Rufford and Samlesbury. Fully three-dimensional stone effigies survive in a rather defaced condition at Clitheroe, Great Mitton, Halsall, Huyton, Kirkland and Ormskirk. The knights at Sefton and Wigan and a lady at Warrington, all of c1290-1335, are probably the oldest of the series. Sefton also has three 16th century brasses, and Warrington additionally has a mid 15th century couple. Caton has a collection of medieval coffin-lids carved with various motifs.

Effigies of the post-Reformation period are also uncommon. Of the early 17th century are couples at Disbury, Eccles, and Farnworth, where there is also an effigy of that period depicting a knight of c1500. Prescot has an upright effigy of c1612, Standish has a recumbent effigy of c1660, Winwick has a late 17th century bust, and Great Mitton has a series of figures from the 1590s to the 1690s, the latter an exceptionally late date for effigies. Flixton has a brass depicting a couple. A brass at Rivington is mostly filled with an inscription but there is a small figure of the deceased shown as a skeleton lying on a mattress. After the Civil Wars of the 1640s monument increasing took the form of tablets set upon the walls. Most of these lack figures other than cherubs or angels but there are sometimes adorned with architectural features such as columns, pediments, etc, and there may also be symbols of death or symbols referring to the profession of the deceased. Good collections of such tablets dating from the 18th century onwards are to be found at Lancaster Priory Church and in Manchester Cathedral. The well-known artists such as Flaxman, Nollekens and Westmacott are all represented by monuments in Lancashire churches, and there are a group of tablets by Webster of Kendal, but none here calls for special comment.

Tomb chest at Bolton-by-Bowland   *Brass at Ormskirk*

Brass of college warden John Huntingdon in Manchester Cathedral

GAZETTEER OF LANCASHIRE CHURCHES

ACCRINGTON   *St James*   SD 760285

This building was erected in 1763 when the town was still just a village. There are galleries on iron columns and two tiers of round arched windows of three lights with the outer lights pointed. The west tower was added in 1806 and the building was enlarged in 1826.

ALTHAM   *St James*   SD 771330

The chancel was rebuilt in 1881 but the rest of the church is late medieval with low windows with uncusped lights in the aisles, and a west tower. Also late medieval is the octagonal font with panels carved with the Instruments of the Passion and the initials I.H.S (for Christ) and M. (for St Mary) The box pews with poppyheads are Victorian. On the chancel south wall is a reset Norman tympanum with rows of small chip-carved St Andrew's crosses.

ARKHOLME   *St John the Baptist*   SD 589719

The church lies at the end of the village with a Norman motte between it and the River Lune. The main body was mostly rebuilt in the 19th century and the north vestry and the south aisle windows and south porch are also of that date. The four bay arcade is late medieval and the aisle east window is 16th century. The bellcote with a segmental pediment is of c1700 although the bell it contains is 14th or 15th century.

ARDWICK   *St Thomas*   SJ 861973

A small church built here to the east of Manchester in 1741 was widened in 1777 and then lengthened by two bays at the east end in 1831. The church is of brick with a flat, deeply coffered ceiling and two tiers of arched windows. It contains three galleries and a 17th century Flemish painting of the Adoration of the Shepherds. In 1836 it was given a distinctive west tower of the Italian campanile type.

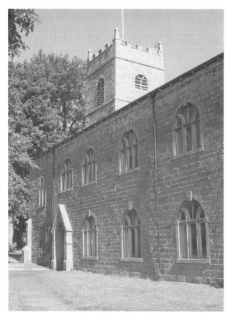

Accrington Church

Altham Church

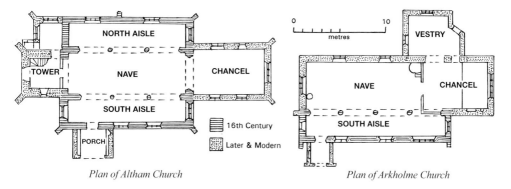

Plan of Altham Church *Plan of Arkholme Church*

ASHTON-UNDER-LYNE *St Michael* SJ 942990

The church was begun in the early 15th century by Sir John de Assheton and completed under the terms of the will of his great-grandson Sir Thomas, who died in 1516. The tower dated from this latter phase but was rebuilt in 1886-8. The north side of the church was rebuilt in 1821 and the south side was rebuilt in 1840-4. The north porch is a memorial of the First World War. The interior of the 1840s is rather fine with panelling over the chancel arch and in the arcade spandrels. The nave and aisles have arcades of five bays, and the chancel chapel arcades are of two bays. There are galleries, box pews and a three decker pulpit with an angel of c1700 at its base. Although none of the windows retain medieval stonework there is medieval stained glass donated by the Assheton family. The glass records Sir Thomas, 1454 and Laurence, rector in 1458. The Postletwaite monument of c1820 is the earliest monument and the oldest in England to have freemasonry emblems.

Arkholme Church

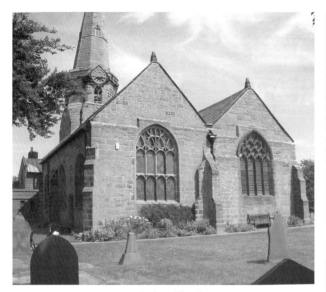

Aughton Church

Barnoldswick Church

AUGHTON   *St Michael*   SD 391055

On the south side are a blocked Norman doorway and an early lancet hardly visible outside. The north aisle with rounded headed windows with intersecting tracery is thought to have been built by a rector of 1528-48 and the north chapel seems to be of about the same date. The arcade with octagonal piers and double-chamfered arches is two or three generations older. There is evidence of an earlier aisle here, narrower than the present one, for the 14th century north tower has chamfered arches towards the nave, north aisle, and north chapel, plus a tomb recess in the north wall. The top is an octagon with broaches and original bell-openings and carries a spire. There are fine roofs in the nave and north aisle with arched braces to collar-beams and wind-braces which in the aisle form elongated quatrefoils. The chancel was rebuilt in 1876. In a recess in the north wall is part of an Anglo-Saxon cross-head with interlace thought to be 9th or 10th century.

BARNOLDSWICK   *St Mary*   SD 893480

This church isolated at the end of a lane has 13th century walling in the undivided nave and chancel with triple east lancets and one other lancet on the north side of the chancel. The diagonally buttressed west tower with a SE stair turret bears a date which looks like 1526. The south aisle with its five bay arcade and straight-headed windows with arched lights is also of about that period, and perhaps the roof and the nave north windows. There are Jacobean box-pews and a three-decker pulpit. See page 6.

BECCONSALL   *All Saints*   SD 453232

The brick old church of 1764 is just two bays long with arched side windows and a Venetian east window. The new church of 1926 by Austin and Paley lies to the west. It has a broad west tower with a pyramidal roof recessed on two sides. See page 9.

BILLINGE   *St Aidan*   SD 533007

A church lay this site in the early 16th century. The present building with pilasters between large round-headed windows is of 1718. At the west end are pairs of pilasters with sections of triglyph frieze and a central doorway with two detached Tuscan columns carrying a projection surmounted by a rotunda with open columns. The interior has a tunnel-vault and four bay arcades of Tuscan columns on high square bases originally hidden by box pews. A tablet by the south wall marked the pew of James Scarisbrick, the Liverpool merchant who initiated the rebuilding. The transepts were added in 1908, whilst the east apse looks like original work possibly moved further east in 1908.

BISPHAM   *All Hallows*   SD 319406

The present rock-faced church of 1883 was designed by John Lowe. The Norman-style south doorway incorporates some genuine Norman stones so the Signs of the Zodiac may reproduce what was there.

East window at Barnoldswick

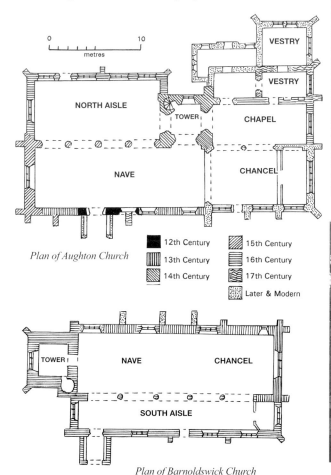

Plan of Aughton Church

■ 12th Century   ▨ 15th Century
▥ 13th Century   ▤ 16th Century
▨ 14th Century   ▩ 17th Century
                  ▦ Later & Modern

Plan of Barnoldswick Church

Billinge Church

BLACKBURN   *St Mary*   SD 684280

A new east end with transepts designed by W.A.Forsythe was added to this church after it was made a cathedral in 1926. Instead of the intended octagonal lantern tower a corona with pinnacles and a spire was added over the crossing by Lawrence King in 1961. The west tower and the nave and aisles were built in 1820-6 to a design by John Palmer but were remodelled after a fire 1831. The only relics of the medieval church and its furnishings are some items of 17th and 18th century plate and eight late medieval stalls with miserichords carved with scenes such as Adam and Eve's Temptation, a fox preaching to geese, an angel with a scroll, an ape and a bearded monster.

BLACKBURN   *St John Evangelist*   SD 684285

The church is of 1789 and has a big west tower with rustication on the square ground stage. The stage above has chamfered edges and then the top stage is octagonal with columns carrying sections of architrave. There are tripartite side windows, the centres having pediments, and an upper tier of lunette windows. There is a Venetian window in the pedimented east wall. A vestry was added in 1865 by J.Bridley and in 1891 the chancel was given giant pilasters and an addition on the south side.

BOLTON   *St Peter*   SD 721093

All that remains of the medieval church and its contents are fragments of Norman carving and some late medieval stalls in the west end of the south aisle. One stall end has angels and a shield and a poppyhead, and there are three miserichords carved with the bust of an angel, a bird in a nest and an acorn with two leaves. There is also the head of an Anglo-Saxon cross. The existing church of 1867-71 designed by E.G.Paley was mostly paid for by the cotton magnate Peter Ormrod. It has aisles with five bay arcades, a large NW tower, transepts and a vaulted chancel. The oldest monuments date from the 1820s.

BOLTON   *St George*   SD 715096

The north and south sides of this brick church of 1794-6 are domestic in character with arched windows and a pediment over the three middle bays out of seven. There is a west tower with a wide doorway. In 1907 James L.Simpson remodelled the interior and added a chancel with a chapel on the south and a baptistry on the north. The concave sided font cover looks like work of c1700. The oldest monument is that of Alice Ainsworth, d1802.

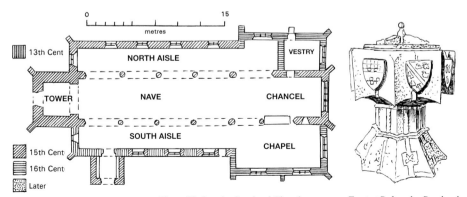

Plan of Bolton-by-Bowland Church   *Font at Bolton-by-Bowland*

St John's Church, Blackburn   *Bolton-by-Bowland Church*

BOLTON-BY-BOWLAND   *St Peter & St Paul*   *SD 786494*

This is mostly a late medieval building with a clerestory over arcades of four bays for narrow aisle. There are wider chapels further east, of one bay with a vestry beyond on the north, and of two bays on the south. There is also a south porch and a fine diagonally-buttressed west tower, whilst there are five light-windows at the east end. The doorway and west window prove the south aisle is of 13th century origin, and also of that period is the priest's doorway. The font of c1510 is octagonal with concave sides with coats of arms and an inscription of brass. Several pews are dated 1694 and there is a panel from a pulpit of 1703, whilst the communion rail is of 1704. The existing pulpit has two old Flemish reliefs set into it. There are brasses of Henry Pudsey, d1509, and his wife, both kneeling. Only the indent remains of second similar brass. On a tomb chest are relief effigies of Sir Ralph Pudsey, d1481, with three wives and twenty-five children in rows below. See p14.

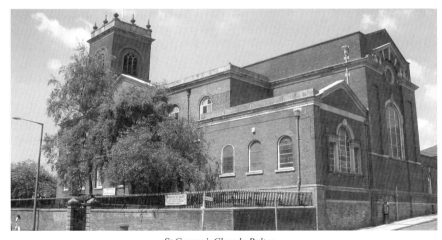

St George's Church, Bolton

Bolton-le Sands Church   *Brindle Church*

BOLTON-LE-SANDS   *St Michael*   SD 484677

The nave has a hammer-beam roof but was otherwise rebuilt in 1813 and remodelled in 1846 when the chancel was rebuilt. Also 19th century are the north aisle and the vestries at either end of it. Original 16th century work are the west tower with diagonal buttresses and a SE stair turret and the north arcade with a rectangular pier between the four bays for the original nave and three bays for the chancel. In the rebuilding the westernmost bay of the chancel became part of the nave, a chancel arch then being inserted. There is an 18th century chandelier and there are two fragments from Anglo-Saxon crosses, one being decorated with interlace.

BRACEWELL   *St Michael*   SD 863485

The south doorway and chancel arch are both Norman work with scalloped capitals on the columns, and the tower may also be 12th century work. An aisle with late medieval windows has a two bay arcade from the nave, and continues into a chapel also with a two bay arcade. The aisle west window, however, is 14th century. The pulpit is Jacobean.

BRADSHAW   *St Maxentius*   SD 736122

The church was rebuilt in 1775 and again by E.G.Paley in 1872. It has transepts and a vestry with a cross-gable. A tower of c1640 of an older church with single small arched belfry-windows stands isolated elsewhere in the churchyard.

BRINDLE *St James* SD 599243

In a rebuilding of 1817 the former north aisle became part of the nave to give sufficient width to accommodate galleries. There are three-light windows with intersecting tracery and transoms. The chancel was rebuilt in 1869-70. Older parts are the late medieval west tower and the north chapel. In addition to the 18th century baluster-shaped font there is an older font which is either late medieval or of the 1660s..

BROUGHTON *St John the Baptist* SD 529344

The ashlar-faced west tower with diagonal buttresses and a SE stair turret is dated 1533. The wide nave with ashlar windows is of 1823 but the thick west wall may represent the west walls of former aisles added to on each face. The medieval church had a south transept, a north chapel of two bays, and an aisled nave of four bays. The chancel and its flanking vestries were added in 1905-6 by Austin & Paley. The chandelier is of 1817.

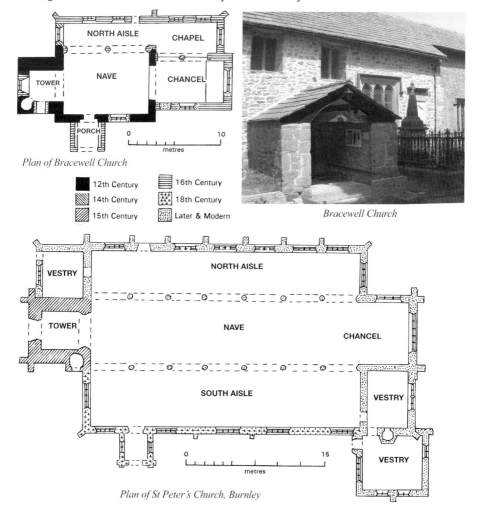

Plan of Bracewell Church

■ 12th Century	▤ 16th Century
▨ 14th Century	▦ 18th Century
▧ 15th Century	▒ Later & Modern

Bracewell Church

Plan of St Peter's Church, Burnley

St Peter's Church, Burnley

BURNLEY   *St Peter*   SD 843330

A church lay here beside the River Don by the 1120s. The 15th century tower with eight pinnacles at the top and a SE stair-turret is the only medieval part. Much work was done on the building in the 1530s but all that remains from that period is the octagonal font carved with a monster, a goat, and the Townley arms. Late medieval in style but not in date are the wide south aisle of 1790 and the north aisle of 1803, although the latter has a Georgian style doorway. There are upper windows for galleries. The arcades with tall slender piers were renewed in 1854 when a clerestory was added and a wooden chancel arch inserted. The big SE vestry is also Victorian. In the south chapel is a 14th century coffin lid with a foliated cross. There are many 19th century monuments to the Townley family. See plan on page 23.

BURTONWOOD   *St Michael*   SJ 565928

A church was built here in 1606 and there is a bench end dated 1610 with the name of Sir Thomas Bold, but the present building of brick with stone dressings was erected in 1716. It has a SW tower and arched windows, the east apse having two of them facing SE and NE. A south aisle with an arcade of Tuscan columns was added in 1939 by E.J.Dod.

BURY   *St Mary*   SD 805109

Nothing remains of the medieval church and its furnishings and the oldest monument is of the 1820s. The west tower with a broach-spire is of 1844-5 and the rest was rebuilt in 1871-6 by Crowther, resulting in a nave and aisles with arcades of four wide bays, a clerestory, chancel, two bay south chapel, and a polygonal apse. There is a fleche over the staircase turret on the north side.

BURY   *St John*   SD 807109

This church consecrated in 1770 now lies derelict. It has sides three bays long and a three bay facade with a truncated gable and two doorways with pediments. There are two tiers of round-arched windows. There is a shallow east apse with a Venetian window. Inside are thin Tuscan columns and galleries.

CATON   *St Paul*   SD 542646

Most of the church, which lies at Brookhouse, is of 1865-7, probably to a design by Paley. The diagonally buttressed west tower is late medieval. In the north aisle west wall is a reset Norman doorway with one order of columns with scalloped capitals and parts of a tympanum with figures thought to be Adam and Eve with the serpent. In the archway are reset several coffin lids with crosses, swords and shears. One has a 14th century inscription referring to the older Roger Burgh. There are monuments to Robert Welch, d1775, and Elizabeth Hodgson, d1795, both featuring a woman and an urn..

CHEETHAM   *St Mark*

The brick church of 1794 has five bays in each direction and two tiers of windows, with three galleries. The chancel was lengthened in 1855 and R.Knill Freeman added the west tower in 1894. For St Luke's Church see page 87.

Burtonwood Church   *Norman doorway at Caton*

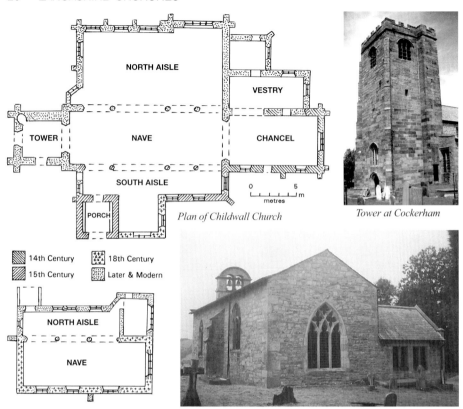

Plan of Childwall Church

Tower at Cockerham

14th Century
15th Century
18th Century
Later & Modern

Plan of Claughton Church

Claughton Church

CHILDWALL   *All Saints*   SJ 415891

This is the only surviving medieval church in the metropolitan district of Liverpool. The 14th century chancel has straight-headed windows of two lights and part of a later window on the north side. The south aisle and porch are 15th century. East of the porch is the Salisbury chapel of 1739-40. In order to clear the view from the family pew in the chapel two of the arcade arches on each side were replaced by a single wide round arch. The west tower with a spire recessed behind an openwork parapet is of 1810-11. The chancel east window also seems to be of that period. The nave was widened on the north side in 1905-6. Fixed on the porch west wall is a fragment of a Saxon cross-shaft with basket ornamentation. On the chancel east wall is a Norman multi-scalloped capital. There is one bench end with a 17th century poppyhead. The box pews are as late as 1851-3. The brass chandelier is of 1737. There are two round arched tomb recesses in the south aisle, which also contains a brass depicting Henry Norris of Speke Hall, d1524 and his wife.

CHIPPING   *St Bartholomew*   SD 622434

The exterior has been completely rebuilt in the 19th century but inside are a 13th century pointed-trefoiled headed piscina decorated with nailhead in the chancel, 14th century arcades of five bays with heads on the capitals, and an octagonal font with concave sides and carvings which is probably early 16th century.

Chorley Church

CHORLEY   *St Laurence*   SD   584177

The ashlar-faced west tower is late medieval but much restored. The nave and aisles are entirely of the restoration of 1859-61, but some old masonry remains in the chancel. It includes a recess in the chancel south wall formerly closed off by bars. This is said to have contained relics of St Laurence brought from Normandy by Sir Rowland Standish in 1442. The Standish family pew with niches, strapwork, caryatids, and a pediment is early 17th century and the Parker family pew with openwork posts with twists is late 17th century.

CHURCH   *St James*   SD 741291

Except for the late medieval west tower the church is of 1804-5 with a flat ceiling, three galleries and two tiers of arched windows. The font with blank tracery is also late medieval. There are two good stained glass windows of 1890 by William Morris in the south aisle.

CLAUGHTON   *St Chad*   *SD 566666*

The earliest feature is the bell dated 1296, the oldest dated bell in England. Of about the same period is the east window of three lights with cusped intersected tracery. This window and the panel dated 1602 at the west end of the small single chamber must be reset for the walls appear to be of 1702. The bellcote must also be of that period. The north aisle with a three bay arcade and the NE vestry plus the south windows are of 1904.

CLITHEROE   *St Mary Magdalene*   SD 754421

The church lies on a ridge with the town between it and the castle. It was entirely rebuilt in 1828-9 by Thomas Rickman except for the west tower with a double chamfered tower arch and the 15th century east window of five lights with panel tracery. Until the rebuilding there was a Norman chancel arch. The octagonal top stage of the tower and the spire with flying buttresses were added in 1844. The front of the altar in the south chapel contains two 17th century panels. There are mutilated effigies of a man and wife of c1440.

COCKERHAM   *St Michael*   SD 463519

This isolated church has a single main body with a clerestory and transeptal chapels and is of 1910 by Austin and Paley, but the ashlar-faced tower is late medieval. See p26.

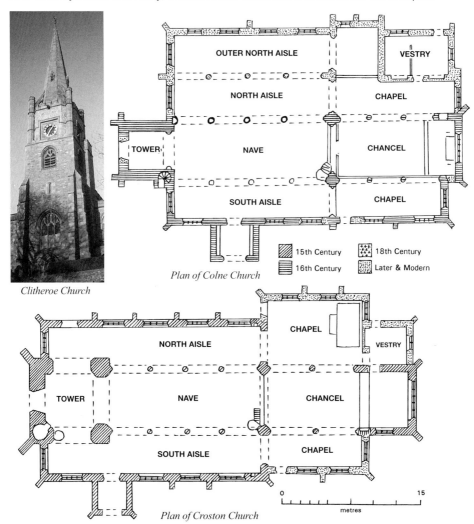

Clitheroe Church

OUTER NORTH AISLE   VESTRY

NORTH AISLE   CHAPEL

TOWER   NAVE   CHANCEL

SOUTH AISLE   CHAPEL

15th Century   18th Century
16th Century   Later & Modern

Plan of Colne Church

NORTH AISLE   CHAPEL   VESTRY

TOWER   NAVE   CHANCEL

SOUTH AISLE   CHAPEL

0   15
metres

Plan of Croston Church

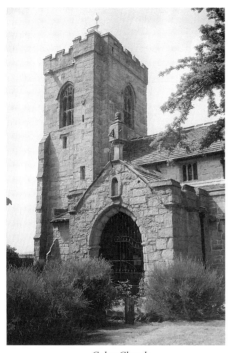

Colne Church

Croston Church

COLNE   *St Bartholomew*   SD 887401

This is essentially a 16th century church with a west tower, aisles with four bay arcades, a wide south porch, and a chancel flanked by chapels with three bay arcades with original screens. The windows are straight-headed with uncusped arched lights. Older are the north arcade of c1200 with circular piers and double chamfered arches and the 14th century south doorway. The whole of the north side is Victorian, an outer aisle being added beyond the north aisle and an organ and vestry beyond the north chapel. The only other Victorian features are the south chapel doorway and the inner order of the tower west doorway. In 1590 Lawrence Townley obtained a font made two generations earlier and gave it to the church. It is octagonal with concave sides and plain shields. The brass chandelier in the nave was obtained in 1773. There are tablets to Christopher Emmot, d1745, and the London merchants John Emmott, d1746, and Richard Emmot, d1761.

CROSTON   *St Michael*   SD 490184

The oldest feature is the 13th century double piscina in the chancel. The west tower has intersecting tracery in the belfry windows and the aisle windows are the same. They cannot be medieval and may be 18th century or of the remodelling of 1823. The arcades of four bays with octagonal piers and double-chamfered arches, and the two bay arcade of the south chapel may be late 15th century. The north doorway with leaf spandrels may be of the same period but the window above it with arched lights under a square head may be part of the work recorded in 1577. The font with quatrefoils is dated 1663. There are old benches in the north aisle.

CULCHETH   *Holy Trinity*   *SJ 662949*

The neo-Norman church at Newchurch looks c1850 but is actually of 1904-5 by Travers and Ramsden. It contains a brass inscription to Elizabeth Egerton, d1646 which is signed by the engraver John Sale, a great rarity.

DARWEN   *St James*   SD 694222

This church of 1722 lies at Chapel Brow. It has a wide and low facade with pilasters and round arched windows along the sides. The Gothic windows and bellcote are of 1850 and the east end was rebuilt in 1937-40. Originally there were three galleries.

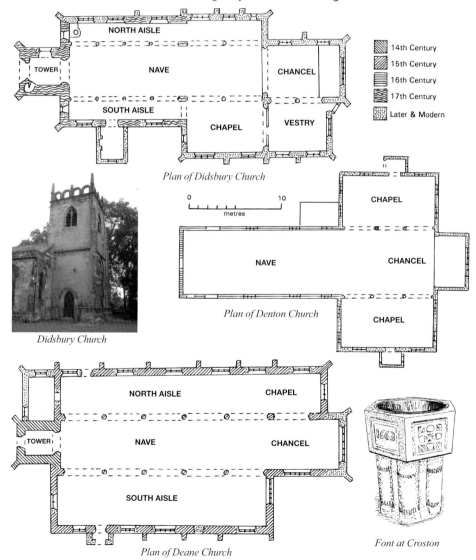

Plan of Didsbury Church

Didsbury Church

Plan of Denton Church

Plan of Deane Church

Font at Croston

Darwen Church   *Deane Church*

DEANE   *St Mary*   SD 693081

The west tower and north doorway are 14th century. Otherwise this is a late medieval church apart from the upper windows inserted to light galleries in the mid 19th century and the lengthening of the chancel in 1884. There are five bays of arcades with low octagonal piers and double-chamfered arches. They may represent more than one building campaign because the capitals at the west end have some decoration including shields whilst the eastern arches on the north side have hollow chamfers. The large brass chandelier is of 1737. No other furnishings or any of the monuments predate the 19th century.

DENTON   *St Lawrence*   *SJ 926951*

This is a timber-framed church built c1530. Original only are the vertical posts of the nave, parts of the roof with cusped wind-braces, some traceried bench-ends amongst the stalls and fragments of reset stained glass, including a number of figures. The chancel with three bay chapels on either side and a sanctuary projecting east are of 1872, with the black and white effect a paint job rather than revealing the structure. There is an oval inscription plate between two columns to Edward Holland, d1655, and of the 18th century are the baluster font and a pew back under the west gallery. See page 8.

DIDSBURY   *St James*   SJ 846904

The west tower with obelisk pinnacles is a relic of the rebuilding of 1620. The columns of the arcades could also be of that period. The church was remodelled in 1855, extended by adding a new chancel in 1871 and the east end of the south aisle rebuilt in 1895. There are kneeling effigies of Sir Nicholas Mosley, d1612, and his two wives and children, plus tablets to Sir John Bland, d1715, and Ann, Dowager Lady Bland, d1736.

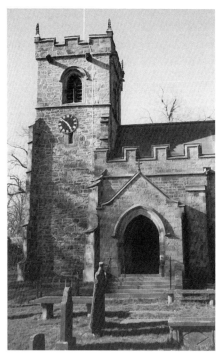

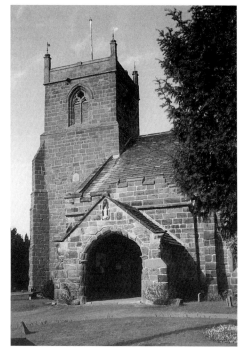

Downham Church   *Eccleston Church*

DOWNHAM   *St Leonard*   SD 784444

The short west tower with diagonal buttresses and a NE stair turret is 15th century and there is a late medieval octagonal font with shields. The rest of the building, comprising a nave with a three bay south aisle with a porch and a chancel with chambers on either side is of the rebuilding by Mervyn Macartney in 1909-10. The brass chandelier was given to the church in 1802.

ECCLES   *St Anne*   SJ 778986

During restorations traces have been found of the Norman church here mentioned in 1180. The earliest surviving part is the early 14th century arch into the south transept. A chantry was founded by Thomas Booth of Barton Hall in 1368. The west tower may date from about the time of the founding of two more chantries by William Booth, Archbishop of York, d1464. When the arcades and the present aisles were built the nave was widened northwards. The aisles are embattled and have windows of 16th century type with panel tracery but were mostly refaced externally in 1907-8. One 15th century window remains in the north aisle west wall. In 1863 a new chancel was added to a design by Holden and the lowest stage of the tower converted into a porch. Built into the eastern end of the north arcade are part of an Anglo-Saxon cross-shaft with knot-work and part of the head of a 15th century lantern cross carved with the Trinity. The early 16th century Flemish stained glass showing the Entry of Christ into Jerusalem in the south aisle west window has come from the church of St John, Deansgate, Manchester. On a tomb chest are recumbent effigies of Richard Brereton, d1600 and his wife, who has alongside her a baby.

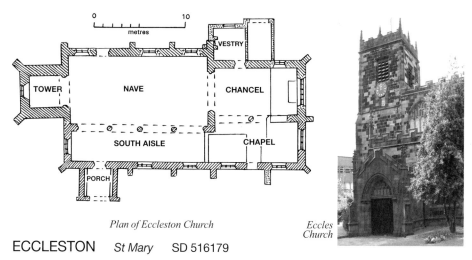

Plan of Eccleston Church

Eccles Church

ECCLESTON   *St Mary*   SD 516179

The church lies by the River Yarrow. The south side is all embattled and the north side has windows of the 1720s given plate-tracery in 1868. The lower part of the tower and the chancel are 14th century, both parts having arches with continuous chamfers towards the nave. The arcades of the south aisle and south chapel probably date from the time of a rector of 1493-1511 who founded a chantry in the chapel. The bell-stage of the tower is late 15th century and so is the octagonal font with quatrefoils containing motifs such as the eagle's claw badge of the Stanleys and the three legs of the Isle of Man, then ruled by the Stanleys. There are a few old bench ends. On a tomb chest is a brass of a late 15th century priest. The best of several tablets is that to the Reverend John Douglas, d1766.

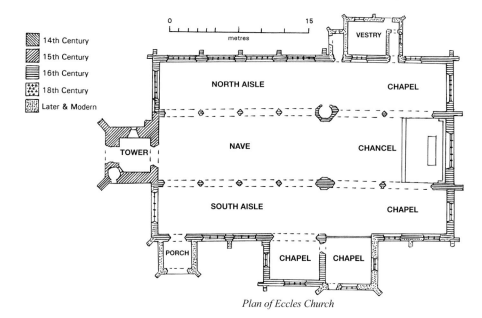

Plan of Eccles Church

Euxton Church

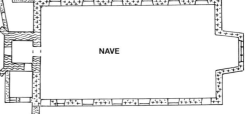

Plan of Edenfield Church

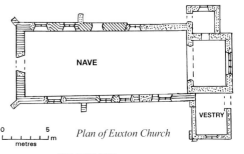

Edenfield Church

0 ⌞ ⌟ 5 m
metres

Plan of Euxton Church

EDENFIELD   *Dedication Unknown*   SD 797197

The west tower is dated 1614. The rest is   of 1778 and has been little altered. There are two tiers of windows, only the lower ones being arched and there are three galleries and box pews in the aisles. The low chancel has a Venetian window.

ELLENBROOK   *St Mary*   SD 726016

This is a brick church of 1725 on the site of an earlier chapel. The windows with two mullions and segmental heads may be later, and in 1842 the neo-Norman chancel and north porch were added.

EUXTON   *Dedication Unknown*   SD 556189

The date on the west front must be 1573, although it looks like 1513. The nave walls and roof with wind-braces may be of that period but the north doorway with continuous chamfers may be 14th century, the windows in the same style are renewed, and the chancel is of 1837 except for the late medieval sedilia. There is a plain 18th century pulpit.

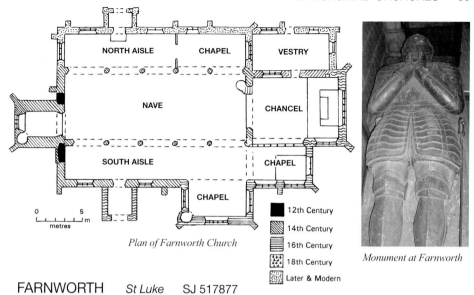

Plan of Farnworth Church

■ 12th Century

▨ 14th Century

▤ 16th Century

▦ 18th Century

▨ Later & Modern

Monument at Farnworth

FARNWORTH   *St Luke*   SJ 517877

The nave west wall contains Norman work. A tower was added in the 14th century and then shortly afterwards new arcades were built, both of them apparently lying northwards of the original walls of the nave. The south doorway is also of that period. The chancel is late 15th century and has a fine panelled roof featuring the griffin badge of the Bold family, but some of the windows at the east end with arched lights are 17th century. The south porch entrance is also 17th century and probably also the timber framed gables of the south transept and chancel, partly hidden behind parapets. The north aisle and arcade and the Bold family chapel north of the chancel were rebuilt in 1892-5. The south transept was built as a private chapel for the inhabitants of Cuerdley by Bishop Smith of Lincoln and has its own west doorway. Reused in the altar is some linenfold panelling from the former transept screen. The tower has a 17th century screen with balusters and 17th century pew ends are reused as wall panelling in the aisle. One panel is dated 1705, and a pew still is use is dated 1602. A bread shelf is dated 1724. The monuments mostly lies in the Bold chapel. The effigy of a knight of c1500 holding a book was probably made in the 17th century. There are alabaster effigies of Richard Bold, d1635, and his wife, and there is a tablet to Peter Bold, d1762. Other monuments of note are 19th century.

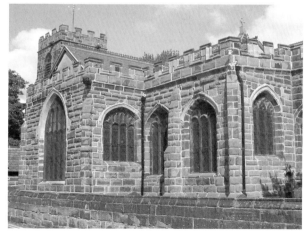

Farnworth Church

FLIXTON   *St Michael*   SJ 747939

One stone from the Norman church here is built into the 15th century east gable of the chancel. The north chapel is Victorian. The west tower was rebuilt in 1731 and the nave and aisles were rebuilt in 1756. Only the east respond remains unrebuilt of the arcade between the chancel and what was a 15th century south chapel until reconstruction in 1815. The nave arcades are Tuscan columns and the windows in the aisles and lower part of the tower arch arched on pilasters. A brass depicts kneeling figures of Richard Radcliffe, d1602, and his wife and children.

FORMBY   *St Peter*   SD 299084

This church of 1746 in Green Lane is of brick with stone quoins. The arched windows are flanked by pilasters. A west projection with lobed sides carries a stone cupola. The chancel is of 1873.

FORMBY   *St Luke*   SD 281067

A Norman font with a rope moulding is the only relic of the medieval chapel destroyed by a sandstorm in 1739. The present building, in woodland west of the station, is of 1852-3

GARSTANG   *St Thomas*   SD 491450

In 1876 a chancel was added to a three bay nave of 1770 with arched windows and a west tower with obelisk pinnacles. The baluster font is dated 1770. See page 11.

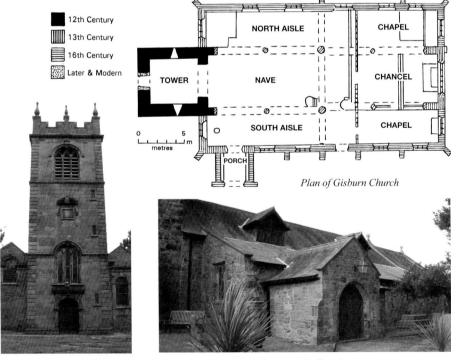

12th Century
13th Century
16th Century
Later & Modern

NORTH AISLE   CHAPEL

TOWER   NAVE   CHANCEL

0   5   SOUTH AISLE   CHAPEL
metres   m

PORCH

Plan of Gisburn Church

Flixton Church   *Goosenargh Church*

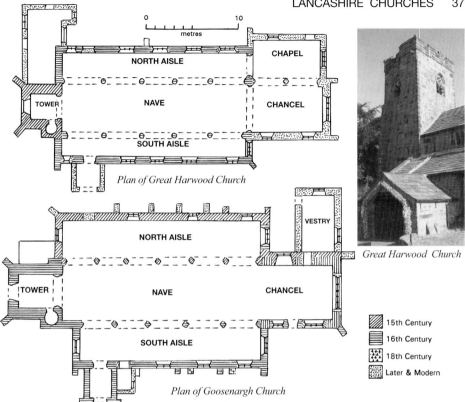

Plan of Great Harwood Church

Great Harwood Church

Plan of Goosenargh Church

15th Century

16th Century

18th Century

Later & Modern

GISBURN   *St Mary*   SD 830489

The Norman west tower retains its original tower arch. Most of the rest is late medieval, an embattled south side with a porch, but the western arches of the two day arcades of the chancel chapels are older than the rest, and the chancel arch itself, plus the south doorway and the west windows of the aisles are late 13th century. There are old screens and two windows contain fragments of 15th century glass. See page 1.

GOOSENARGH   *St Mary*   SD 560370

The very thick north wall of the chancel may be partly 13th century and there are three small lancets in the east wall. The north aisle contains a tomb recess containing a 14th century slab with tracery and shields appropriated in the early 17th century by one of the Rigby family. The six bay arcade and north windows look 15th century, whilst the south aisle with a five bay arcade probably dates from the rebuilding of 1553, and the west tower may also be of that date. There is no chancel arch. The screen to the north chapel is dated 1622 and 1721 and the tower screen is dated 1678. The brass chandelier is 18th century

GREAT HARWOOD   *St Bartholomew*   SD 737323

The squat diagonally-buttressed west tower may be 15th century. The low nave and aisles with square-headed windows with arched, uncusped lights are early or mid 16th century. The chancel seems to have been rebuilt in the 19th century, and the north chapel and south porch are of that date, whilst the NW vestry is more recent.

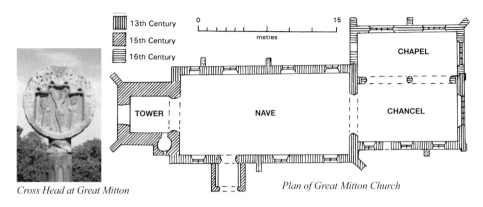

Legend:
- 13th Century
- 15th Century
- 16th Century

TOWER   NAVE   CHANCEL   CHAPEL

Cross Head at Great Mitton   *Plan of Great Mitton Church*

GREAT MITTON   *All Hallows*   SD 715390

The wide nave and the chancel are both of c1300, with a five-light east window, sedilia, and two-light side windows with Y-tracery. The diagonally-buttressed west tower with a SE stair-turret is early 15th century. The fine screen has a inscription referring to an abbot of Sawley. The font cover is dated 1593, and there is a pulpit which is partly of c1680, and partly early 18th century. Medieval tracery is reused in the screen dividing off the north chapel of 1594 which contains a defaced medieval effigy of a knight and a fine series of monuments to the Sherburnes of Stoneyhurst. There are recumbent effigies of Richard, d1594, and his wife, and kneeling effigies of their son Richard and his wife, plus Richard, a boy, d1702. Of the 1690s, and thus amongst the last recumbent effigies to be made before they were revived in the 19th century, are the figures of Richard, d1667, Richard, d1689, and his wife Isabel, d1693, plus another Richard, d1690. See page 11.

Monument at Great Mitton

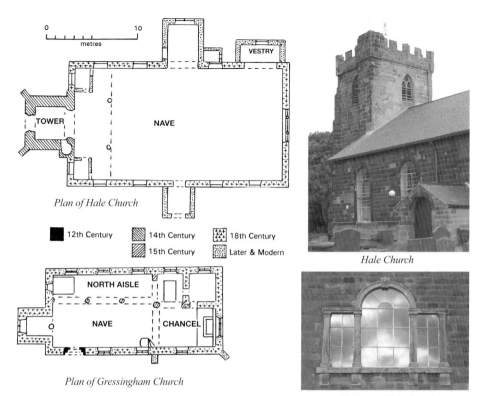

Plan of Hale Church

12th Century   14th Century   18th Century
15th Century   Later & Modern

Plan of Gressingham Church

Hale Church

Window at Hale Church

GREAT SANKEY   *St Mary*   SD 568885

The brick nave with a polygonal west end containing the font is of 1768-9. The chancel was rebuilt by William Owen in 1834 and the bell-turret is of 1865. The nave windows have been Victorianised.

GRESSINGHAM   *St John the Evangelist*   SD 573699

The church consists of a nave with a north aisle, a west tower, and a chancel flanked on its north side with a small chapel now containing a Victorian tomb and a vestry. The exterior was entirely rebuilt in 1734 when the tower was added, and the box pews may be of that date. Only the tower west window has remained unaltered as the result of a remodelling by Paley in 1862. The south doorway is Norman and has three orders of arches with chevrons and a rope moulding. Probably of the 16th century are the three arches of the north arcades and the arches towards the chapel from the chancel and aisle. One of the panels of the pulpit is dated 1714. At the SW corner is an ancient stone carved with a trail and in the vestry are two fragments from an Anglo-Saxon cross with scrolls. The head has seven blobs in the middle. See page 5.

HALE   *St Mary*   SJ 471820

The west tower is 14th century. The main body is of 1754 but only the west gallery survived the remodelling of 1875. There is a Venetian window at the east end. The tablets include one to Ireland Aspinwalle, d1733.

Halsall Church

Haslingden Church

HALSALL   *St Cuthbert*   SD 371103

The vestry doorway and the traceried door it contains plus a nearby recess in the chancel north wall are 14th century, as are the four bay arcades with octagonal piers and arches with sunk quadrants and the south aisle east window with fragments of original glass. The sedilia and piscina belong to a 15th century remodelling of the chancel when the two rood-stair turrets were provided. The west tower with an octagonal upper stage with broaches and then a spire is of the turn of the 14th and 15th centuries. There is a late 16th century window on the south side which once gave light to the pulpit. There are late 15th century stalls with miserichords and bench ends with poppy-heads and tracery. An alabaster early 14th century effigy of a priest lies under a recess which may be still earlier. The former school room at the SW corner is dated 1695 but may be a century older.

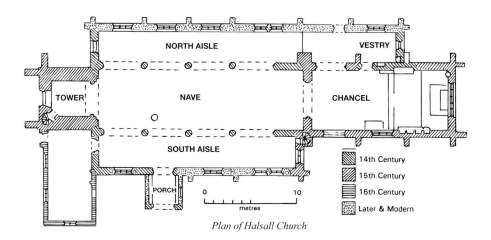

Plan of Halsall Church

Halton Church

Cross at Halton

HALTON   *St Wilfrid*   SD 498647

The west tower is said to have once been dated 1597 but probably contains older work. Much of the church was 14th century until the rebuilding of 1876-7 by Paley and Austin removed the medieval parts. Their church has a north aisle only. In the churchyard are reset fragments of an 11th century cross with various scenes and Signs of the Evangelists, plus the mid 18th century family vault of the Bradshaws built against a slope.

HASLINGDEN   *St James*   SD 785236

The church is of 1780 and has seven bays of arched windows in two tiers. It was enlarged in 1827 when a lofty diagonally-buttressed west tower was added. The octagonal font with shields is early 16th century. The galleries were remodelled in the late 19th century

HEAPEY   *St Barnabas*   SD 602205

In 1865 transepts and a chancel were added to a nave with arched windows with mullions and transoms probably of the mid 18th century, although a date up to a century earlier is possible. Further work seems to have been done here in 1829.   See page 10.

HEATON CHAPEL   *St Thomas*   SJ 883927

The white rendered nave with arched windows is of 1765. Tracery was inserted into the windows c1875, and then in 1937 Bernard A.Millar added a west porch and a square chancel of brick. There are several memorial tablets, but none of importance.

HEYSHAM   *St Peter*   SD 410626

The church lies at the end of the village overlooking the sea. Perched on a rock to the west are ruins of a tiny 8th century chapel of St Patrick. A south doorway with the jambs converging towards the top is the only surviving feature. Nearby are contemporary graves cut into the soft sandstone. The church itself consists of a small nave flanked by two bay aisles, and a chancel flanked by a two bay chapel on the south and a single bay chapel and a vestry on the north. The blocked west doorway is Saxon (another Saxon doorway lies by the path to the chapel) and the chancel arch with rope mouldings on the capitals is probably no later than 1100. The chancel of c1300 has original windows to the south and east, the former now looking into the chapel and the latter having cusped intersecting tracery. Between the chapel and chancel is a 16th century arch containing a contemporary screen. The south aisle may be 14th century although the arcade looks later and the south chapel and porch are probably 16th century. The north aisle is of 1864. The small

porch projecting from the vestry has stones with the dates 1677, 1668, 1699, 1705, and 1720, but it is uncertain what they relate to. The double bellcote is 17th century and so is the font cover. There are two fragments with scrolls from Saxon crosses. More important is the lower part of a cross outside carved with foliage scrolls and depicting a gabled building with arched niches or windows. There are busts in these and there is also a swathed figure. On the other side is a seated figure with a halo. See page 4.

Interior of Heysham Church

Heysham Church

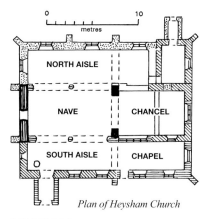

Plan of Heysham Church

Hindley Church

HINDLEY   *All Saints*   SD 623043

There was a chapel-of-ease here to Wigan church. It became Presbyterian after the Civil War but reverted to the Anglian church in 1690. The present brick structure four bays long by two bays wide was erected in 1766 and has a gallery of 1776, the north and south galleries being later Georgian. The arched windows have glazing bars in the form of three stepped pointed lights.

HOLLINS GREEN   *St Helen*   SJ 697912

The main body of the church and the cupola are of 1735, but most of the details are of the remodelling of 1882.

Heysham: chapel plan

HOLME   *St John*   SD 876285

The 1897 the nave of 1788-94 was remodelled inside and a chancel and vestry added. The church is of ashlar and has a bell-turret with an octagonal cupola. Older relics, all early 16th century, are the Flamboyant style pierced panels in the pulpit, a few bench ends, and some linenfold panelling.

HOOLE   *St Michael*   SD 463323

The small brick nave of 1628 has mullioned windows with arched lights and a south porch with a segmental shaped entrance arch with leaf spandrels, a very late instance of their use. The tower added in 1722 straddles the west wall, the east corners being supported inside by large detached columns. The large polygonal font has an inscription with the date 1663. Several bench ends and parts of the desk are 17th century and the pulpit has a tester dated 1695. There are galleries on the west and south sides and box pews.

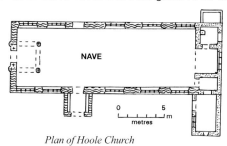

Plan of Hoole Church

Hoole Church

Tower at Hornby

Apse at Hornby

HORNBY   *St Margaret*   SD 585686

The aisle outer walls are of 1817 and the arcades of five bays plus a single much wider bay on each side for chancel chapels are of 1889. The NE vestry goes with the latter. The other parts are relics of a church begun in 1514 by Sir Edward Stanley, Lord Mounteagle, and left incomplete at his death in 1524. At the west end is an octagonal tower, the second stage of which is twisted so that its angles coincide with the middles of the sides of the lower stage. At the east end is a polygonal apse with angle buttresses and two light windows, although the east window is wider and has three lights. Polygonal apses and towers which are octagonal from the ground are very rare in English parish churches. The cross-shaft fragment with chevrons may be Norman, whilst another fragment with two fishes, loaves of bread and two figures either side of a tree, plus much interlace and a half figure on the other side, is Anglo-Saxon. Yet another fragment has on each side an arch on shafts.

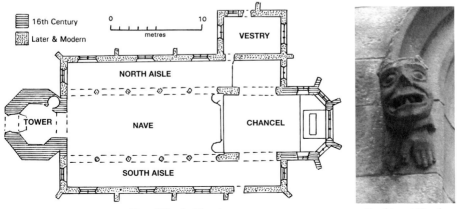

Plan of Hornby Church   *Headstop at Hornby*

HUYTON *St Michael* SJ 442912

The reset south doorway and the south arcade with double-chamfered arches on octagonal piers are 14th century. Both aisles were rebuilt in 1815-22, that on the south being made wider. The west tower is 15th century but the top, with obelisk pinnacles, is dated 1664. The priest's doorway and hammerbeam roof of the chancel look 17th century. There is a Norman font with primitive heads in arcading and a frieze of rosettes above, and the is a late medieval font with pointed quatrefoils and shields. The fine screen of c1500 has Flamboyant tracery. An inscription, now lost, told of how the screen was taken down during the rebellion of 1647 but restored and replaced in 1663.There is Flemish woodwork of 1700 in the chancel. The defaced alabaster effigy of a priest may depict John de Winwick, who founded a chantry here c1380. His brother founded a second chantry.

Font bowl at Huyton

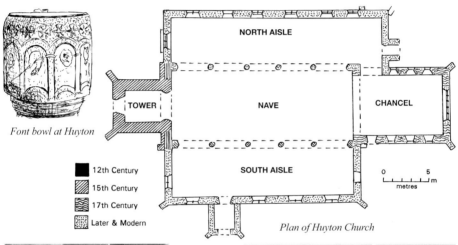

■ 12th Century
▨ 15th Century
▧ 17th Century
▨ Later & Modern

Plan of Huyton Church

Priest's doorway at Huyton

Huyton Church

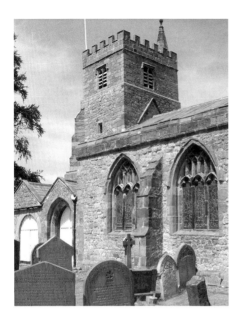

KIRKBY   *St Chad*   SJ 409990

The tub shaped Early Norman font is carved with seven saints, Adam and Eve with the serpent, the Angel of the Expulsion and St Michael spearing a serpent which goes round the underside of the bowl like a rope-moulding, and there are fat roll-mouldings on the stem and base. The medieval chapel-of-ease here was replaced by a Georgian chapel which in turn was in 1869-71 replaced by a fine church designed by Paley and Austin with a central tower capped by a saddleback roof.

KIRKHAM   *St Michael*   SD 427324

In 1843-4 a fine tower and spire in the Decorated style designed by Edmund Sharpe was added to a nave of 1822 with tall lancets between buttresses. The chancel was built in 1853. The only older relics are the brass chandelier of 1725 made by Brown of Wigan and the 14th century tomb recess with pierced tracery in the south aisle.

Kirkland: two views

13th Century
14th Century
15th Century
16th Century
18th Century
Later & Modern

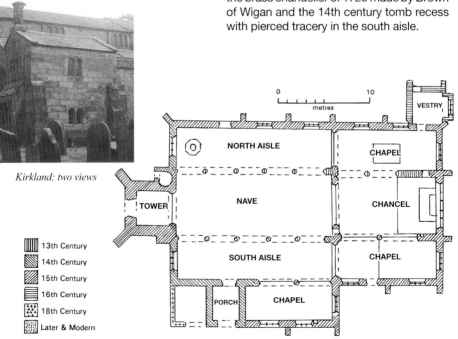

Plan of Kirkland Church

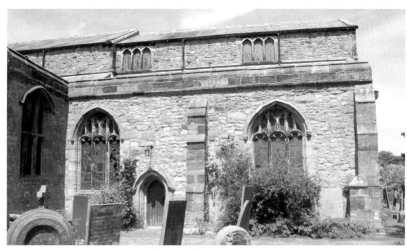

Kirkland Church

KIRKLAND   *St Helen*   SD 482428

This the original parish church of Garstang. The earliest part is the north chapel arcade of the 1230s. The north aisle arcade is only slightly later. The south aisle of c1300 has cusped intersected tracery in its west window. The north aisle west window is similar but later. Of the 15th century are most of the other windows and the west tower with a little spire over its stair turret. The two storied vestry is probably mid 16th century. The clerestory windows are of 1811. In the south chapel is a piscina of c1300. This part has a ceiling dated 1529 and the chancel roof is dated 1620. The pulpit with arabesque panels looks Elizabethan but is actually of 1646. The south chapel screen is 17th century in its lower parts. The nave has an 18th century brass chandelier. There is a defaced medieval effigy.

Lancaster: Priory Church

LANCASTER   *St John*   SD 477619

In 1754 Harrison added a west tower to a nave of 1754-5 with five bays of arched windows. There is also an apse with two windows. The tower has bell-openings with pilasters and pediments and a rotunda of attached Tuscan columns surmounted by a spire, upon which is a fish weather-vane. The nave has a coved ceiling and three galleries with unfluted Ionic columns. The box pews and communion rail are original but the pulpit is of 1875.

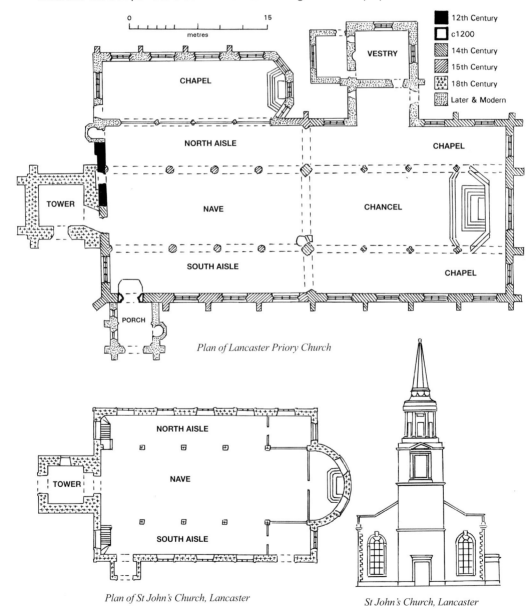

Plan of Lancaster Priory Church

Plan of St John's Church, Lancaster

St John's Church, Lancaster

LANCASTER   *St Mary*   SD 474619

Roger de Poitou founded a Benedictine priory on the hill beside his castle in 1094. There seems to have already been a church on the site for a Saxon doorway survives in the nave west wall and excavations in 1912 revealed footings of an 11th century apse just east of the present chancel arch. The south doorway with one order of columns and continuous mouldings is 13th century. The nave has a 14th century west doorway now looking into a tower of 1754 by Sephton on the site of a 15th century one. The eastern parts of the church seem to be late 14th century and the rest dates from about the time when the church was transferred to the control of Syon Abbey near London in the 1430s, Henry IV having severed the connection between priories in England and mother houses in France. The south side is all embattled and has seven bays, the buttresses having polygonal ends and the windows four-centred arches with cusped and stepped lights. The east window of five lights has panel tracery. The arcades have four bays either side of the chancel arch, making eight bays in all. In 1903 Austin and Paley added the two storey south porch with a stair turret and the outer north aisle with a polygonal apse. See page 47.

The very fine set of 14th century stalls with miserichords are said to have been brought here from either Cockersand or Furness. The canopies are the most ornate in England with tracery like the French Flamboyant style of c1500. The pulpit is dated 1619. The stairs to the west gallery are 18th century. The three large brass chandeliers with two tiers of arms are dated 1717. In the north chapel are a collection of Anglo-Saxon carved stones from various crosses. One has vine and scroll patterns, another depicts Adam, Eve and the serpent, plus the Crucifixion, another has Christ in a circle, and others show two birds and two human figures, a hart and hounds with snakes, and an inscription to one Cynibad. No medieval monuments survive, the oldest monument being the tablet with a bust of Sir Samuel Eyre, d1698. There are other monuments to William Stratford, d1753, the six-year-old Sibyl Wilson, d1773 and Frances Atkinson, d1779, whilst outside in the churchyard is a monument of c1790 to the Rawlinson family.

Interior of Lancaster Priory Church

LATHOM   *Dedication Unknown*   SD 456094

Set in a group with some almshouses is a chapel of c1500 built by the second Earl of Derby to serve the inhabitants of his fortified house which lay to the east. Only a doorway and parts of the screen have escaped restoration. The lectern may also be old.

LEES   *St John the Baptist*   SD 955045

The nave with a cupola and two tiers of windows was built in 1742 and given two more bays at the east end in 1772. H.Cockburn in 1865 renewed the galleries and altered much of the rest, creating a chancel by inserting piers in the east bays.

LEIGH   *St Peter*   SD 666003

The late medieval west tower has been refaced externally but the tower arch is genuine and has the mark of the former medieval nave roof above it. The rest is in the late medieval style with an embattled clerestory running the length of the building but is the work of Paley & Austin in 1869-73, replacing a fully aisled building eight bays long. At the SE corner is a vestry door set diagonally. They added a choir vestry on the north side in 1910.

LEYLAND   *St Andrew*   SD 541215

There is a reset Norman capital on the south side of a chancel of c1300 with later sedilia and piscina and intersecting tracery in the east window. The lofty west tower is 15th century. These parts are now connected by a nave of 1816-17 with three galleries on thin iron columns. There is a tablet and a bust to Sir William Farrington, d1781.

LITTLEDALE   *St Anne*   SD 559623

The Welch family had this church erected in 1752-5. There are three bays with windows of two arched lights under a basket arch. The building is now a private house.

Leigh Church   *Lowton Church*

Leyland Church

LIVERPOOL   *Our Lady and St Nicholas*   SD 340905

This is the parish church of Liverpool and was founded c1360 as a chapel-of-ease to Walton. Nothing remains of the medieval chapel nor anything of another still-older chapel nearby known as St Mary-at-Kay. The existing church was built in 1952 to a Gothic design by Edward C.Butler, the church of 1811-15 by Thomas Harrison having been destroyed by bombing during the war except for the tower with a spire on a recessed octagonal stage with flying buttresses connecting the spire to angle pinnacles.

LIVERPOOL   *Holy Trinity*   SD 352899

This classical style church of 1790-2 has a west tower with concave angles to the top stage. There are two tiers of windows, one round arched and the other segment arched. Vestries adjoin the short chancel with a Venetian east window. Inside are three galleries and a flat ceiling.

LOWTON   *St Luke*   SJ 616977

The brick church is of 1732 with arched windows with keystones and Y-tracery. There are transepts containing galleries, with two lunette windows on the south. The chancel has Venetian windows. The west tower is of 1863. There are box pews and a baluster font.

Former church at Littledale

Old church remains at Maghull

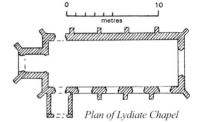

Lydiate Chapel

Plan of Lydiate Chapel

LYDIATE *St Catherine* SD 364049

This ruined building has a nave and chancel, neither of which have north windows. It was probably built by Lawrence and Catherine Ireland of Lydiate Hall in the 1470s since their initials appear over the outer arch of the south porch. The south and east windows appear to be of that date. The west tower had a west arch tall enough to include a window over a doorway. A chalice and a series of fine alabaster panels showing the life of St Catherine now fixed to a pulpit remain in the Catholic church of 1854-5 to the NE

MAGHULL *St Andrew* SD 385020

The new church of 1878-80 designed by J.F.Doyle is rock-faced with a west tower. Of the old church only the late 13th century chancel and north chapel now survive. Between them is a two bay arcade with double-chamfered arches and a circular pier. The small east window in the chapel has intersecting tracery. An old doorway has been reused in the wall built after the nave of c1830 was taken down, and bell-turret of that period was then re-positioned.

MANCHESTER *St Anne* SJ 837984

This church was built in 1709-12 at the expense of the Lady Ann Bland, together with the adjoining square. The west tower originally had a three stage cupola. The six bays have two tiers of round-headed windows with coupled pilasters below and coupled strips above. The apse has giant Corinthian pilasters. The choir in the nave was created during the restoration by Waterhouse in 1886-91. Original furnishings include part of a three-decker pulpit with angle columns, the wrought iron rail being once part of the communion rail, box pews, and a font with an octagonal bowl on a baluster stem.

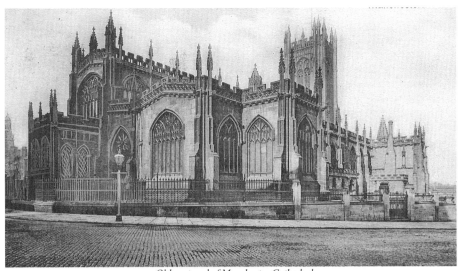

Old postcard of Manchester Cathedral

St Anne's Church, Manchester

Interior of Manchester Cathedral

MANCHESTER   *Cathedral Church of St Mary, St Denys & St George*   SJ 838987

The church here is mentioned in Domesday Book but nothing so early now survives. It became a cathedral in 1847. Rector Thomas de la Warre was licensed by Henry V in 1421 to refound the church as a college for with a warden, eight priests, four clerks, and six lay choristers. The college buildings some distance to the north still survive since they became the Chetham Hospital in the 17th century. The first warden John Huntingdon (1422-58) rebuilt the east end of the church. His rebus appears upon a beam in the chancel ceiling and his brass lies in the middle of the floor (p15). The nave was rebuilt by Ralph Langley, third warden (1465-81) and various alterations were made by John Stanley, Bishop of Ely and fifth warden (1485-1509), whose brass lies in the Derby Chapel. The west tower lies slightly south of the axis of, and probably predates, the nave with its six bay arcades. The chancel also has six bay arcades and then there is seventh bay forming a Lady Chapel, rebuilt after bomb damage during the Second World War. The piers and arches (mostly renewed) are far from homogenous, no less than seven different designs being evident.

Chantry chapels were added in profusion around this core, resulting in what looks like a wide outer north aisle to the nave and a still wider outer aisle to the choir, the Derby Chapel founded by Bishop Stanley c1513. On the south side more chapels create the appearance of another outer aisle to the nave. There are two storey porches two bays deep on both sides. Flanking the south side of the south choir aisle from west to east are the Jesus Chapel endowed as a guild chapel in 1506 and later used as a vestry and library, the chapter house with a polygonal south front and a fine panelled north entrance, and the Fraser Chapel added in 1886. The Ely Chapel projecting north from the Derby Chapel was not rebuilt after destruction by war-time bombing. There is a very high tower arch and their are fine old roofs with angel-busts and bosses in the nave.

The west porch and vestries are of 1898 by Basil Champneys and his also designed the south annex of 1902-3. There was a restoration in 1814-15 and then in 1862-8 J.P.Holden mostly rebuilt the tower, heightening it by 6 metres. He also rebuilt the Jesus Chapel. The pierced parapets around the church are the result of another restoration by J.S.Crowther in 1885-6. He also renewed the arcades so that not much medieval masonry now survives.

In the choir are the very fine stalls provided by Bishop Stanley c1505-10. They have two tiers of canopies, and a cresting with segmental arches on pendants. The front stalls have poppyheads with animals and grotesques curving up to them. On the south side the miserichords have the Stanley arms and show, from the east: a rabbit cooking a hunter, a unicorn, a cock and cockatrice in combat, a venerer and stag, a stag and hound, the fox's triumph, men playing backgammon, a child fighting a dragon, a winged lion, a man with a broken cooking pot, monsters in combat, a pelican and a bust of an angel. On the north side the miserichords have the merchants's mark of Richard Beswicke and show from the east: a gryphon, an antelope, a sow playing bagpipes with pigs dancing, a lion passant, bear-baiting, a man robbed by monkeys, a fox stealing a goose, men on a camel fighting a unicorn, the elephant and castle, a shield, a dragon, an eagle, and an eagle and child.

The brass chandeliers in the choir were given in 1690 and 1715. There are remains of late medieval screens in the choir and in the arcades of the Jesus chapel and the Derby chapel, and there are screens and a communion rail of 1750-1. The rood screen erected by Bishop Stanley was restored and given a parapet by G.G.Scott in the 19th century. The respond of the north arcade has a reset piece of Anglo-Saxon sculpture with a small relief of an angel. In addition to the brasses already mentioned there others of c1460 to Sir John Byron and his wife (very fragmentary) and to Anthony Moseley, d1607, and Oswald Moseley, d1630, and their wives. There are also many 19th century monuments.

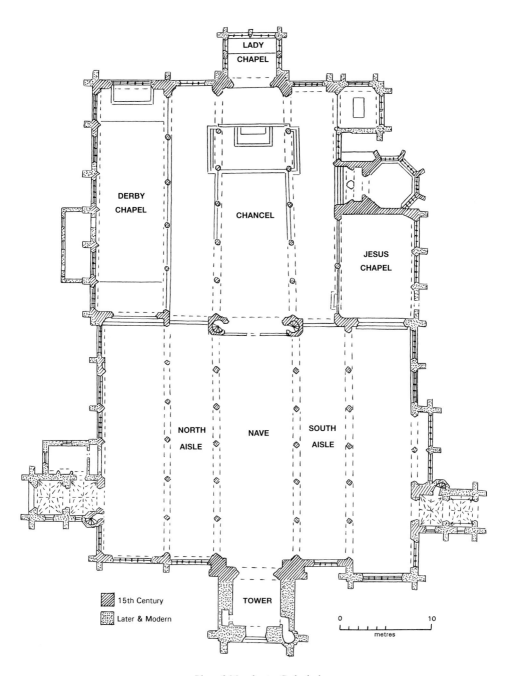

Plan of Manchester Cathedral

Melling Church

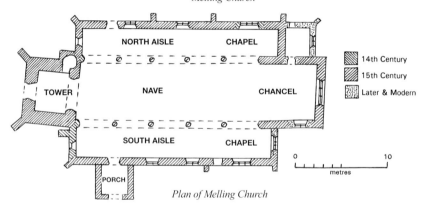

NORTH AISLE   CHAPEL

TOWER   NAVE   CHANCEL

SOUTH AISLE   CHAPEL

PORCH

14th Century

15th Century

Later & Modern

0   10

metres

Plan of Melling Church

MELLING   *St Wilfred*   SD 598711

Most of the church is 15th and 16th century. It has aisles with arcades of five bays and a diagonally buttressed west tower having a NE stair turret, being set at an awkward angle to the nave. There is no chancel arch. Older parts are the western responds of the arcades, the south aisle west window, and a larger three light window on the north side, all 14th century. Still older relics are fragments of two cross-slabs, one with a circular plait and the other with interlace, and the lower part of what may have been a small 13th century crucifix. The NE vestry and the chancel east and south windows are the only Victorian parts, although a clerestory added in 1763 was then also remodelled. Part of the dado of the medieval screen remains, although not in situ. There is a 17th century baluster screen in the tower arch. The benches in the north aisle are also 17th century. The oldest of the monuments is a cartouche of 1735 to young Sandford Marsden.

MIDDLETON   *St Leonard*   SD 872063

Of the church consecrated by Bishop Langley of Durham in 1412 there remain the west tower with diagonal buttresses, the south porch with niches either side of the outer arch and presumably some walling in the south aisle. It was probably then that the original Late Norman chancel arch of three pointed orders with chevrons and multi-scalloped capitals was reset to serve as the tower arch. The arcades of octagonal piers with double-chamfered arches are thought to be part of the work executed for Richard Assheton in the 1520s, there being a datestone of 1524 on the south aisle parapet. His arms appear on the dado of the screen which forms the only division between the nave and chancel. The chapels on either side of the chancel also probably date from this period, as do the stalls in the chancel with eight miserichords. Probably of the 1660s are the weatherboarded top stage of the tower and the vestry east of the Assheton chapel on the south side. The vestry parapet may, however, be reused early 15th century work. The Assheton chapel has a reset 13th century doorway. The east window is of 1847. There is a Victorian vestry north of the north chapel. Other vestries east of that chapel and projecting beyond the north aisle doorway are more recent. See page 58.

In the south aisle is the Hopwood Pew, a late 17th century piece with twisted balusters. The chancel south window contains fragments of stained glass with kneeling donors, relics of a window commemorating the English victory over the Scots at Flodden Field in 1513. There is an empty tomb recess in the north aisle. In the chancel are brasses depicting Sir Richard Assheton and his wife, Edmund Assheton, Rector of Middleton, d1522, Alice Lawrence and her two husbands, Richard Assheton, d1618, and his wife and Ralph Assheton, d1650, and his wife.

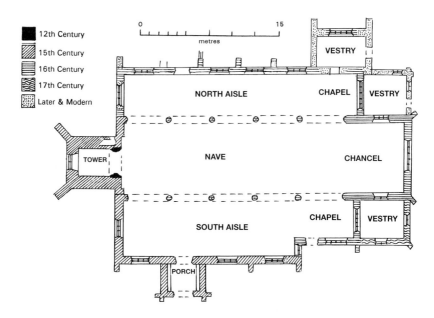

Middleton Church

Middleton Church

NEWCHURCH-IN-PENDLE   *St Mary*   SD 823394

The short west tower is dated 1653 but may be a century older. The main body of the church seems to be of 1740, the date appearing over the blocked priest's doorway. There are round arched south windows and a Venetian east window. The north aisle with a four bay arcade of Doric columns may also be 18th century but perhaps of the 1780s rather than 1740. The aisle has two tiers of windows for it contains a gallery, and there is a west gallery in the nave, which has a brass chandelier of 1756 with two tiers of arms.

NORTHENDEN   *St Wilfred*   SJ 833901

Only the screen of the 1520s remains of the original church, although the existing building of 1873-6 by Crowther is reported to be similar to what stood there before. It has a west tower, a nave and aisles of five bays with piers with castellated capitals, and a chancel flanked by two bay chapels. The 18th century font has a tiny bowl on a baluster stem. The monuments include tablets to Robert Tatton, d1689, and an urn to Mrs Egerton, d1784.

NORTH MEOLS   *St Cuthbert*   SD 365186

The church lies at Churchtown and is mostly of 1730-9, with a west tower with a spire and a contemporary font and bench ends, although the diagonally buttressed SW corner looks medieval. The south porch is dated 1909, and a restoration of that period by Isaac Taylor removed all traces of a remodelling of 1860, provided a new chancel, and moved the original Venetian east window to a new location on the north side.

Venetian window at North Meols Church

Newchurch-in-Pendle

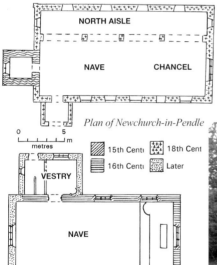

Plan of Newchurch-in-Pendle

Plan of Old Langho Church

Old Langho Church

OLD LANGHO   *Dedication Unknown*   *SD 701358*

A 13th century piscina and four 15th century windows from Whalley Abbey are reset in this single chamber probably of the 1550s. The communion rail is probably of the 1630s. There are fragments of old glass in the SE window, and there are 17th century bench ends with shields and dates. In 1879 the building was superseded by the new church of St Leonard at Billington by the main road 1km to the SE, which was designed by Paley & Austin.

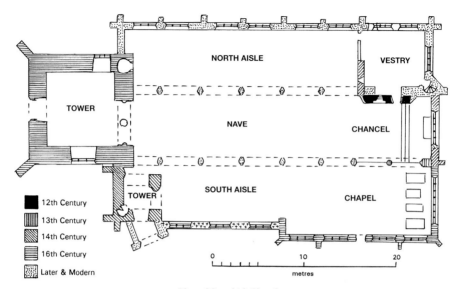

Plan of Ormskirk Church

ORMSKIRK   *St Peter and St Paul*   SD 413084

The oldest feature is a Norman window in the chancel north wall. The two bay arcade of the south chapel is late 13th century. The eastern two bays of the south aisle once formed a 13th or 14th century transept. A south aisle must have existed when the south tower was built probably in the late 14th century. It has an octagonal top rising from a square base. The south arcade is mostly the work of Paley and Austin in 1877-91, when much of exterior of the church was restored, but it seems to represent an arcade of the 1540s, which is the period of a huge second tower at the west end. It has pairs of three-light bell-openings with uncusped intersecting tracery. Prior to the restoration the north arcade, at least, was a classical affair of 1729. The Derby Chapel on the south side of the chancel is thought to be an addition of 1572. It has a 17th century screen with high balusters. The chapel contains mutilated effigies of two knights and their wives, all of c1490-1500. One may be the 1st Earl of Derby, whose second wife was the mother of Henry VII. There are also two tomb chests with quatrefoils on the sides and indents of brasses of late 15th century couples on the lids. In the south aisle is a life-sized brass of a knight of the Scarisbrick family, c1500. The font of 1661 is carved with a pelican, a cross, an hourglass, a crown and the initials of Charles II. On the east wall outside is a panel showing two men which may be Saxon. In the churchyard is an 18th century sundial. See pages 10 and 14.

OVER KELLET   *St Cuthbert*   SD 522696

The west tower and the north aisle are 16th century. The west bay of the south arcade is of c1200. The west respond of the north arcade also seems to be of this period and may have originally been the eastern respond of the south arcade. The narrow south aisle and the east end were rebuilt in 1863-4 and also of that period are the north porch and the NW window with one late medieval reset window. The rebuilding has removed any former south doorway and that on the north is closer to the east end than is usual. See page 6.

Overton Church

Ormskirk Church

OVERTON   *St Helen*   SD 440575

In 1771 the east end was rebuilt wider and a north transept added long enough to contain vestries beyond a family pew. Until then the church consisted of a small single chamber. Not much of the walling is now medieval but the south doorway is Norman with chevrons on two orders of arches, the bellcote may be 13th century and in 1902 foundations of a Norman east apse were discovered during a restoration by Austin and Paley. The 18th century pulpit and tester are partly sunk into the thickness of the south wall. See page 7.

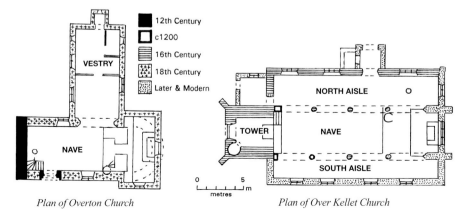

12th Century
c1200
16th Century
18th Century
Later & Modern

VESTRY

NAVE

NORTH AISLE

TOWER   NAVE

SOUTH AISLE

0   5
metres   m

Plan of Overton Church   *Plan of Over Kellet Church*

OVER WYRESDALE   *Christchurch*   SD 551545

The church is of 1733 and has quoins and two typically Georgian south doorways. The tower is of the same date although it looks older. In fact the only older feature is the pulpit dated 1684. The chancel, nave windows and spire are all additions of 1894.

PENWORTHAM   *St Mary*   SD 524290

The church lay between a motte and bailey castle on the end of the ridge and a small Benedictine priory. The chancel with a single-framed roof is early 14th century, and although the windows are restored they contain fragments of original glass, whilst the tower is 15th century. The nave was rebuilt by E.G.Paley in 1855. In the south aisle is a font of 1667. The two helmets are thought to have belonged to John Fleetwood, d1590.

PILLING   *St John the Baptist*   SD 403486

The old church of 1717 has five bays with windows with a mullion running up to the apex of an arch and a double bellcote with a segmental pediment. The east window has two mullions. The box pews are original and also the three decker pulpit. The upper tier of lunette windows on the north side were inserted in 1812-3 to light a new gallery. The new church not far to the north is of 1886-7 by Paley and Austin. It cost £7,000 and has a west tower with a recessed spire, arcade piers which are octagonal with concave sides and chancel chapels of differing shapes and sizes.

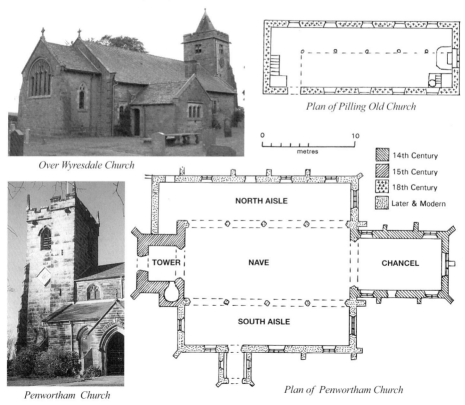

Plan of Pilling Old Church

Over Wyresdale Church

0   10
metres

▨ 14th Century
▨ 15th Century
▨ 18th Century
▨ Later & Modern

NORTH AISLE

TOWER   NAVE   CHANCEL

SOUTH AISLE

Penwortham Church

Plan of Penwortham Church

Poulton-le-Fylde Church

Doorway at Pilling

POULTON-LE-FYLDE   *St Chad*   SD 348395

In 1604 it was reported that the chancel had collapsed, and the oldest features surviving now are the diagonally buttressed 17th century west tower, a screen dated 1636 in the south aisle and a pulpit of that period with arabesques. The tower doorway is of 1752-3, like the rest of the church, which has two south doorways with Tuscan columns, triglyphs and pediments. Above them are horizontally-placed oval windows. The Y-tracery of the large arched windows may be later. There are three galleries, that on the west having a fine staircase, and there is a brass chandelier d1710 in the sanctuary. Positioned where one would expect the priest's doorway to be is the Fleetwood family vault with a doorway dated 1699 surmounted by a broken pediment on corbels.

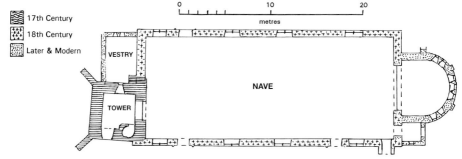

Plan of Poulton-le-Fylde Church

PRESCOT   *St Mary*   SJ 465927

The west tower with pilasters on the bell-stage is of 1729, but the spire is later 18th century. The aisles with windows with intersecting tracery are of 1819-20 but inside are plaques dated 1620, the probable date of the nave roof and the five bay arcades with thin octagonal piers. The chancel retains some medieval masonry. There are stalls with poppyheads dated 1636, a communion rail of about the same period, and a font of 1755. There is an upright effigy of Sir John Ogle, d1612. The earliest tablet is that to Thomas Barron, d1751. See pages 10 and 12.

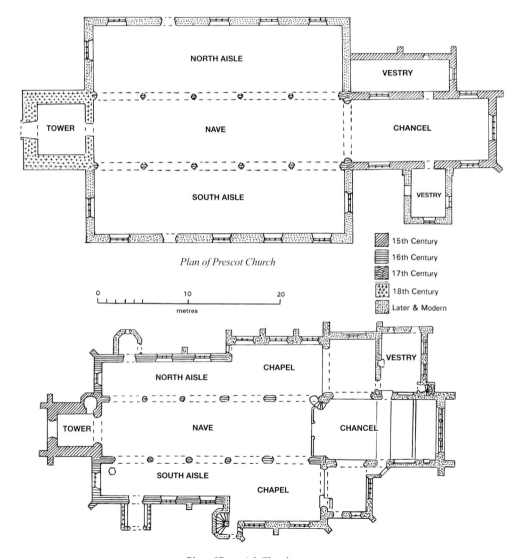

Plan of Prescot Church

15th Century
16th Century
17th Century
18th Century
Later & Modern

0   10   20
metres

Plan of Prestwich Church

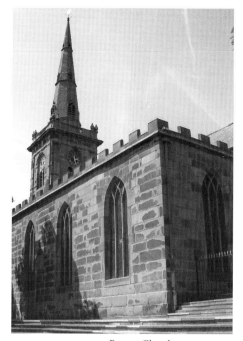
Prescot Church

Prestwich Church

PRESTON   *St John the Divine*   SD 542294

Originally dedicated to St Wilfred, this church was founded c900. The town was granted a charter in 1179, and there must have been a substantial building here by the 13th century. It was rebuilt in 1581 and again in 1770 after part of it collapsed. Old illustrations depict an embattled building with a four-light window with intersecting tracery on the south side of the chancel. As rebuilt again in 1853-5 by E.H.Shellard the church has aisles containing galleries, hammerbeam roofs, and there are chancel chapels of three bays. The only pre-Victorian relics are the 16th century lowest part of the tower, a late medieval font with quatrefoils, heads and a stem with eight column, a brass dated 1623 to Seth Bushell, and a number of memorial tablets. The oldest two, both in the chancel, are to Mrs Broughton, d1715, and Dame Mary Hoghton, d1720.

PRESTWICH   *St Mary*   SD 812037

The west tower is 15th century. The arcades seem to have been heightened in the late 16th century or early 17th century, probably reusing 14th century material since the north aisle west window is of that date. There is a clerestory above the arcades. The aisles have windows with cusped lights and then a tier of three light mullioned windows above, presumably of the date of the arcade heightening. The plain walling included in the fourth piers from the west seems to be a relic of a former aisle-less chancel, and the third pier on the north, also with a bit of blank walling, shows where the chancel arch once was. The present chancel with two chapels on the south and a chapel and two storey vestry with a turret on the north were added by Paley and Austin in 1888. The south porch is dated 1756 and the brass chandelier must also be of that period.

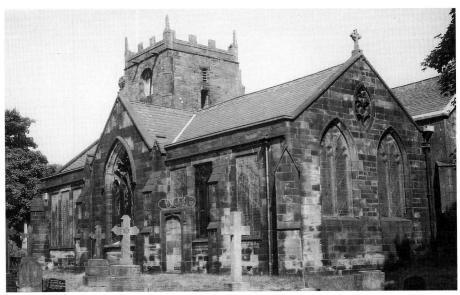

Radcliffe Church

RADCLIFFE   *St Mary*   SD 797076

The church lies at Church Green, 1km east of the centre. The chancel arch is 14th century. The arcades of two bays are early 16th century, the roof bosses and clerestory also being of that date. The north transept has 14th century masonry but the south transept is swallowed up by a wide south aisle of 1870-3 by J.M. & H.Taylor. The chancel was rebuilt in 1817. The tower arch looks late medieval but the tower itself with diagonal buttresses with many set-offs is dated 1665. Seats at the nave west end are dated 1606 and 1665, although the panels with the former date have come from a pulpit. Under the altar is an early 16th century alabaster slab incised with effigies of James de Radcliffe and his wife.

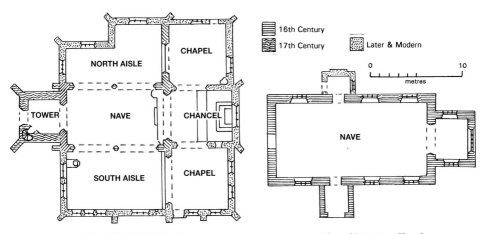

Plan of Radcliffe Church   *Plan of Rivington Church*

Wall painting at Ribchester

Ribchester Church

RIBCHESTER   *St Wilfred*   SD 649350

The church lies on the site of a Roman fort. It has a fine 13th century chancel with one south lancet and three stepped east lancets. Another lancet is reset in the 14th century north chapel with a trefoil-shaped arcade pier and three original windows. Also 14th century are the south doorway and the west tower with a similarly moulded doorway, plus the octagonal buttressed font. Much of the south aisle and the parts of the screen that have escaped restoration are 16th century. The windows in the aisle and chancel with geometrical tracery are Victorian. The pulpit looks Elizabethan but is dated 1636. There are box pews dated 1735 and 1761. Two of the Tuscan columns of the west gallery are said to be reused Roman work. In the north aisle east window are fragments of old glass. In the porch is a plain 15th century tomb chest carved with shields.

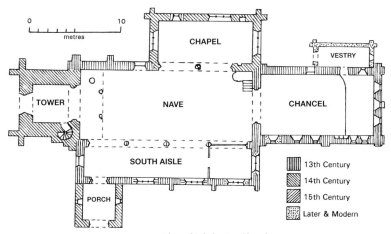

Plan of Ribchester Church

RINGLEY   *St Saviour*   SD 764052

Only the very thin tower remains of the church of 1625. The church of 1850-4 by Sharpe and Paley lies in the same churchyard. It has a nave, chancel with lancets, and a SW turret and contains two early 19th century monuments to the Fletcher family. See page 9.

RIVINGTON   *Dedication Unknown*   SD 625144

The straight-headed windows with arched, uncusped lights date from c1540 and so must the linenfold panels of the pulpit and the surviving old parts of the screen. Other plain mullioned windows probably date from the rebuilding of c1666. There is a fine 18th century chandelier with two tiers of arms. There is a brass with an inscription to John Shawe, d1627, who is depicted at the bottom as a skeleton on a mattress. The bell house by the west gate of the churchyard seems to have existed by 1611. See pages 9 & 66.

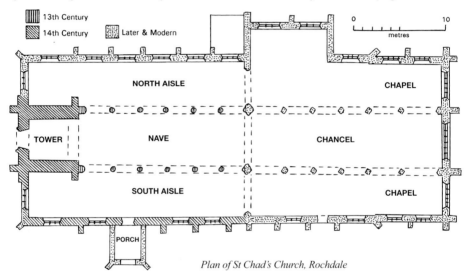

Plan of St Chad's Church, Rochdale

St Chad's Church, Rochdale

Rivington Church   *St Mary's Church, Rochdale*

ROCHDALE   *St Chad*   SD 897132

The arcades of six bays between the nave and aisles are 13th century, the piers being alternately circular and octagonal, and the arches double-chamfered. The eastern piers have broaches at the springing of the arches, whilst the western piers have capitals with leaves and heads. The lofty tower arch is 14th century. In the 1850s the north aisle was rebuilt by Joseph Clarke. The south aisle was rebuilt in the 1870s, when the present south porch was erected and the tower was heightened with the addition of an elaborate bell-stage. In 1883-5 J.S.Crowther lengthened the chancel, the two bays east of where the side chapels have diagonal buttresses on the former SE and SW corners being his work. He also designed the present chancel arcades of six narrow bays.

Parts of the stalls and screens are medieval with heraldic panels. The communion rail in the south chapel with twisted balusters is late 17th century. This chapel became the burial place of the Dearden family c1847 and it was then that the alabaster slab to the 14th century rector John Dearden and brasses to other members of the family were made. There are many 19th century monuments but the only older one is the fluted urn with pilasters and a pediment to James Hole, d1712.

ROCHDALE   *St Mary-in-the-Baum*   SD 895136

As built in 1740 this brick church had a nave and aisles with arched windows between pilasters and galleries. In 1909-11 Sebastian Comper dramatically remodelled the church, retaining the north aisle as an outer chapel. The old nave became a north aisle to a higher new late-Gothic style nave where the south aisle once was. A lofty arcade divides the old and new naves in stark contract to the lower arcade with Tuscan columns between the old nave and its former north aisle. The old aisle had its windows lengthened and a balustrade was added. Only the pulpit remains of the original furnishings, the screens being part of Comper's work..

RUFFORD   *St Mary*   SJ 464157

A chapel in the village existed in 1346 and was rebuilt in 1746. The present building of 1869 was designed by Dawson and Davies. It is of brick, with a steeply pyramidal-roofed NW tower and plate tracery and bar tracery in the windows. It contains a chandelier of 1763, a small brass of a knight, and an incised slab depicting a knight and wife of c1460. There is also a tablet by Flaxman to Sophia Hesketh, d1817.

ST HELENS   *St Thomas Becket*   SJ 499971

None of the town centre churches are ancient but in the Windle Hall cemetary 2km to the NW lies the tower of a chantry chapel of St Thomas Becket founded by Sir Thomas Gerard c1435. Low walls, mostly rebuilt, outline the former nave and chancel.

ST MICHAEL'S-ON-WYRE   *St Michael*   SD 463410

Much of the church is 16th century, money being left in a will of 1549 for "the building of the steeple", although the existing tower seems to be later. The low embattled south aisle has windows with uncusped lights. Of narrow 13th century aisles there remain two bays on the north, with a doorway, and a blocked west window and adjoining arcade respond on the south. The wider eastern two bays on the north are early 14th century, one window having fragments of original glass. Also of that period is the wall-painting of the Ascension on the chancel north wall, whilst the chancel east window is late 14th century.

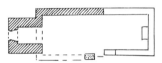

Windle Hall Chapel: plan & view

Samlesbury Church

SALFORD   *Sacred Trinity*   SJ 834987

The west tower is either early 18th century or goes back to when the church was founded in 1635. The west window and bell-openings are of the time of the restoration by Holden in 1871-4. The church itself is of 1752 and has two tiers of arched windows, three galleries with Tuscan columns and doorways with rustication.

SAMLESBURY   *St Leonard*   SD 590303

The undivided central body is of 14th century origin and has a renewed west window with intersecting tracery. The aisles with four bay arcades and the clerestory may be as late as the enlargement of the church recorded in 1558. The communion rail, the two decker pulpit and many of the pews are 17th century. The pews have dates from 1678 to 1756. The helm belonged to one of the Southworth family. In a north window are fragments of old stained glass. There is an incised slab depicting Sir William Atherton and his wife who died in 1441.

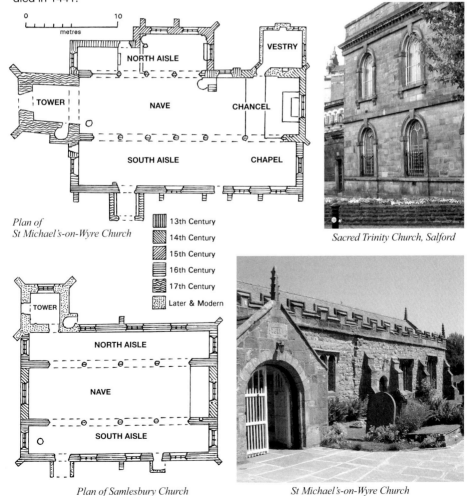

Plan of St Michael's-on-Wyre Church

||| 13th Century
14th Century
15th Century
16th Century
17th Century
Later & Modern

Sacred Trinity Church, Salford

Plan of Samlesbury Church

St Michael's-on-Wyre Church

SEFTON   *St Helen*   SD 356014

The north chapel with an original piscina and the west tower are 14th century. The pinnacles are probably of c1802 when the spire needed repair after being damaged by a gale. The tower east wall shows traces of a 14th century nave roof well below the height of the present one. The north aisle west wall retains traces of a 14th century aisle narrower than the existing late 15th century aisle. The six bay arcades, the south aisle with windows with uncusped lights, the clerestory, the two storey porch with leaf spandrels at the outer entrance and the chancel sedilia and piscina and with windows with two transoms are all 16th century. Members of the Molyneux family were rectors in 1489-1509 and 1535-7 and their arms appear on the porch.

The church contains a very fine set of 16th century screens, the rood screen having putti (a Renaissance feature) on the dado. Other screens surround the Sefton pew, which is not in its original place. The initials of Rector James Molyneux appear on the stalls with poppyheads. There are poppyheads on the bench ends which have carved motifs including letters of the alphabet. The communion rail and tower screen have twisted balusters of the 1690s, originally probably all part of one three-sided communion rail. The chapel communion rail is Jacobean. There is a font cover dated 1688 on the octagonal late medieval font with quatrefoils. The pulpit with arabesque decoration and a tester is dated 1635. The two large brass chandeliers were given in 1773. In a tomb recess in the north chapel is an effigy of a late 13th century cross-legged knight in chain-mail. There is another cross-legged knight of c1330. Under the chapel arcade are two plain tomb chests with quatrefoils and shields. Placed in one of them are brasses of Sir Richard Molyneux, d1568, and his two wives and children. In the chapel is a brass of Margaret Bulcley, d1528, daughter of Sir Richard Molyneux. A brass to him, d1548, and his two wives lies in the chancel.

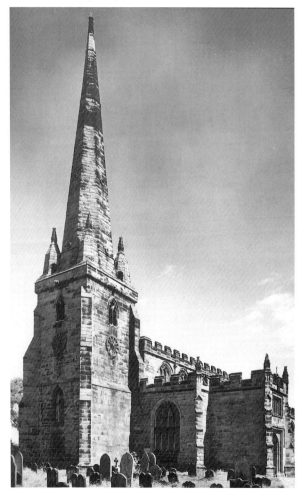

Sefton Church

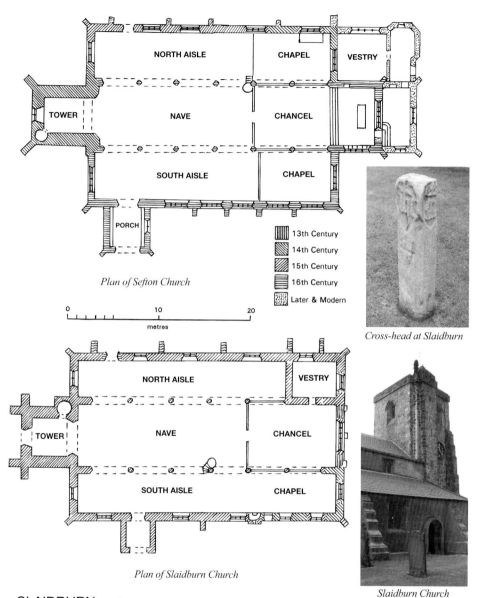

Plan of Sefton Church

13th Century
14th Century
15th Century
16th Century
Later & Modern

0   10   20
metres

Cross-head at Slaidburn

Plan of Slaidburn Church

Slaidburn Church

SLAIDBURN   *St Andrew*   SD 710521

This is a fully aisled church with a clerestory over arcades of six bays, a rood-loft staircase and porch on the south side, and a west tower with angle-buttresses and a NE stair-turret. Most of it is late medieval but one window betrays the south chapel as 14th century. The windows are mostly straight-headed with arched and cusped lights. The chapel screens and roofs are medieval also, but the main screen closing off the chancel is Jacobean and the font cover is of c1590. The box pews and three-decker pulpit are 18th century.

Roof at Standish Church

Standish Church

STANDISH   *St Wilfred*   SJ 563103

The west tower with an octagonal stage is of 1867 and the low vestries at the east end are of 1913-4 by Austin and Paley. The rest of the church seems to be all 16th century. It consists of a nave and chancel of equal width flanked by aisles of five bays and chapels of two bays with the chancel extended one further bay to the east. The arcades have Tuscan columns but the arches may be 14th century work reused. The church seems to be the work of several campaigns and we cannot be sure what was built when. Money was spent on rebuilding in 1539, yet the church was "in grete ruyne" in 1544. Further rebuilding took place in 1557-8 and in 1582-4. Still surviving is a contract dated 1582 between Rector Richard Moodie and the mason Robert Charnock. The date 1584 appears over the north chapel arcade, whilst the south chapel is thought to be of 1589. Turrets containing stairs to the former rood-loft mark the join between the arcades of the aisles and chapels. One would normally expect these to be no later than the 1530s since rood-lofts went out of fashion after the Reformation. The pulpit was given in 1616, although it looks Elizabethan. There are bench ends dated 1625 and 1626 and a communion rail made from the balustrade of a staircase of a house in Wigan. The Purbeck marble effigy of a 14th century priest was appropriated monument to Richard Moodie, d1586, an inscription and tomb chest being added. On a tomb chest is a fine recumbent alabaster effigy of Edward Wrightington, d1658. Edward Chisnall died in 1653 but his tablet with trophies and putto heads looks a generation later than that. See page 13.

STYDD *St Saviour* SD 653358

The chapel originally belonged to a preceptory of the Knights Hospitallers. The doorway in the west wall probably allowed access from the preceptory onto a balcony at that end. On the north side are two Norman windows and a doorway with a chamfered round arch. The south doorway with waterleaf capitals is early 13th century, whilst the east window with intersecting tracery and the west window with Y-tracery are of c1300. Two south windows with straight heads and the font with shields are late medieval. The pulpit and screen with balusters are 17th century. See page 7.

TARLETON *St Mary* SD 451204

In 1824 an oblong brick tower with a stone rotunda with a cap was added to a brick box of 1719 which is four bays long with a canted apse. The font is 18th century. There is a west gallery and a half gallery on the south.

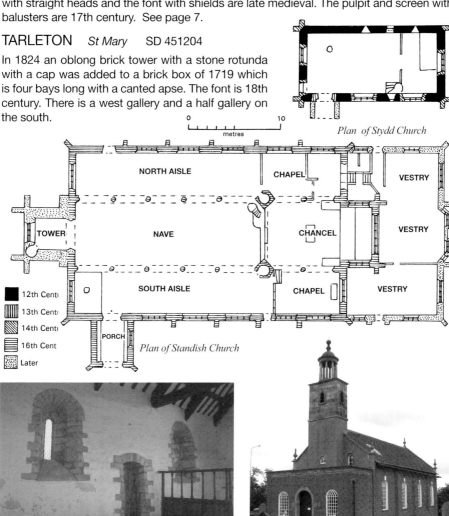

Plan of Stydd Church

Plan of Standish Church

12th Cent.
13th Cent.
14th Cent.
16th Cent.
Later

Interior of Stydd Church

Tarleton Church

TATHAM   *St James*   SD 605694

The Norman south doorway has one order of colonettes with multi-scalloped capitals. The east end of the single chamber with large blocks and a plinth at the SE corner must be of c1300, with an east window with intersecting tracery and sedilia and piscina on the south side. The three bay arcade is 16th century. The aisle west window and doorway are also of that period but the windows there, and along the south side, plus the NE vestry, date from a drastic restoration by Paley & Austin in 1885-7. They put a saddleback roof on the west tower of 1722 and added a porch with a reused medieval outer arch and a Norman window reset in its east wall.

TUNSTALL   *St John the Baptist*   SD 614739

Arcades of four bays, the coarse windows in the south aisle, the two-storey south porch and the west tower with diagonal buttresses and a NE stair turret may represent the work executed for Sir Thomas Tunstall c1415. The responds of the north aisle have 13th century capitals and the west windows of the narrow aisles could also be of that date. The north aisle windows look 14th century. Of the 16th century are the east window containing old glass donated c1810, and the south chapel with a single wide arch continuing the line of the older south arcade. In the chapel is an old effigy. The arch on the north side towards the organ and the vestry projecting north beyond the organ space are Victorian but the church has escaped the drastic restoration which was normal for Lancashire churches.

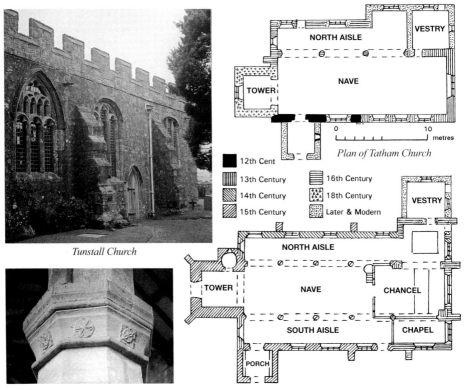

Tunstall Church

Plan of Tatham Church

12th Cent
13th Century
14th Century
15th Century
16th Century
18th Century
Later & Modern

Capital at Tunstall

Plan of Tunstall Church

Font at Tunstall

Upholland Church

UPHOLLAND   *St Thomas*   SD 523051

The nave and aisles with arcades of tall slender piers are 14th century work and originally formed the east end of the church of a priory founded in 1317 by Walter de Langton, Bishop of Lichfield. A chapel here endowed ten years before by Sir Robert de Holland has not survived. The aisle windows are renewed. At the west end can be seen the east piers of the intended crossing tower and arches which would have opened into transepts. These parts do not seem to have been built and a broad west tower was built on the site of the intended crossing c1500. A new chancel was added in 1882-6 and this contains a late 17th century communion rail of twisted balusters. The nave has a plaster ceiling of 1752 and contains a few bench ends of 1635, whilst the churchwardens pew is dated 1679. One south window contains some old stained glass.

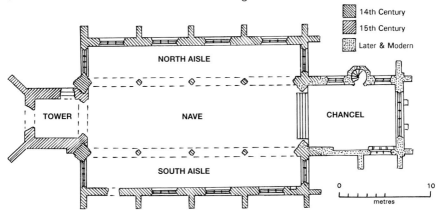

14th Century
15th Century
Later & Modern

NORTH AISLE

TOWER   NAVE   CHANCEL

SOUTH AISLE

0   10
metres

Plan of Upholland Church

WADDINGTON   *St Helen*   SD 728438

Much of the church, which has aisles and chapels with uninterrupted arcades of five bays, dates from a rebuilding in 1901, but the chancel has an old piscina and of the 15th century are south doorway, the south aisle west window and the west tower with angle-buttresses, a NE stair-turret, and a west doorway with nine heads over the rere-arch. Also of that period is the octagonal font with shields showing the Instruments of the Passion. The benches in the north chapel are of c1590-1620.

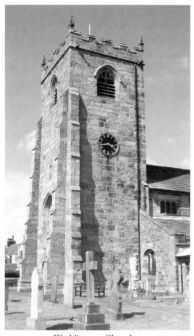

Waddington Church

WALTON   *St Mary*   SJ 359949

Until 1699 this was the parish church of Liverpool. The Norman font is carved with the Flight into Egypt, St John the Baptist, and Adam and Eve, and there is a fragment of an Anglo-Saxon cross-shaft. The church itself was entirely rebuilt in 1828-32 to a design by John Broadbent. The quatrefoiled windows date from then. The north side was remodelled in 1840 with close-set buttresses. The south chapel is of 1911 and the south aisle may then have been remodelled. The interior is all quite modern.

WALTON-LE-DALE   *St Leonard*   SD 561281

In 1902-5 a wide nave designed by J.P.Seddon was erected between the west tower and low chancel which are both 15th century, although the chancel has a reset 13th century priest's doorway. There is blank panelling above the chancel arch. The church contains many minor tablets, mostly to the Hoghton family. See page 80.

Font at Waddington

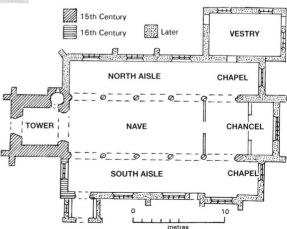

Plan of Waddington Church

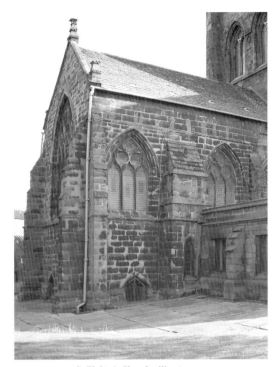

St Elphin's Church, Warrington

Holy Trinity Church, Warrington

WARRINGTON   *St Elphin*   SJ 610885

The dedication is a rare one. The church lies at the east end of the old town and is now mostly the work of Frederick and Horace Francis in 1859-67. Loose fragments survive of a Norman church. The chancel is partly 14th century and stands on a crypt of that date. The crypt vault is Victorian but the head corbels are original. More 14th century work remains in the east and north walls of the north transept including two tomb recesses. There is a spire on the central tower, which is of 1696 upon neo-13th century piers of the 1860s. The wide nave and wide aisles are now all 19th century, although the south aisle with its upper tier of windows for a gallery is of 1835 rather than the 1860s. In the north transept are a defaced early 14th century female effigy, and a tomb chest with statuettes of angels and saints plus recumbent effigies of Sir John Boteler, d1463 and his wife. The Patten family chapel once lay west of the south transept, into which their many monuments have been transferred. They include tablets to Thomas, d1772, and Dorothea, d1799. Outside in the churchyard is a sarcophagus to William Hesketh, d1773, and John Hesketh, d1793.

WARRINGTON   *Holy Trinity*   SJ 606882

This Gibbs' style church in Sankey Street is of 1760 with a tower added in 1862 by W.P.Coron. There are two tiers of windows, the uppermost having keystones and flanking pilasters, whilst the lower have Gibbs surrounds. There are box pews and three galleries with a fine staircase to the western one. A chandelier from the House of Commons was given to the church in 1801.

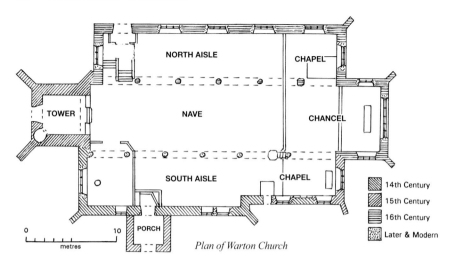

Plan of Warton Church

14th Century
15th Century
16th Century
Later & Modern

0 ——— 10 metres

WARTON   *St Oswald*   SD 498723

The oldest parts are the 14th century south chapel with sedilia and a priest's doorway and the contemporary south aisle with its doorway, two original windows and bold corner buttresses. It is just possible that these parts were originally the nave and chancel and that a new nave was added on the north side in the 15th century when a south porch and west tower with diagonal buttresses were added and the south chapel east end rebuilt. The south arcade is 19th century. The north aisle and chapel with an arcade of six bays in all and the chancel east end are 16th century, but only the chancel south window and the unusually wide north doorway have escaped being renewed. One pew has set-in shields and there are bench ends dated 1571 and 1612 now in the rectory. The font is of 1661.

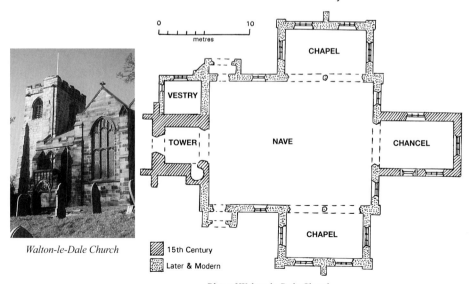

Walton-le-Dale Church

15th Century
Later & Modern

Plan of Walton-le-Dale Church

Warton Church

WAVERTREE   *Holy Trinity*   SJ 392891

In 1911 Sir Charles Reilly added buttresses of an odd obelisk shape and an east bay and apse to a nave built in 1794 by John Hope. Hope's church has lofty north and south galleries and the upper stage of the west tower has a lantern. The tower base now contains a vaulted baptistry. The pulpit and lectern are of the 1970s.

Wavertree Church

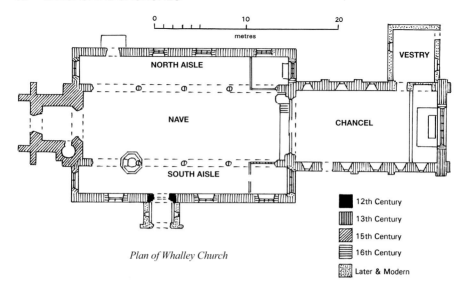

Plan of Whalley Church

12th Century
13th Century
15th Century
16th Century
Later & Modern

WHALLEY   *St Mary*   SD 733361

The nave and aisles with arcades of four bays of double chamfered arches on circular piers on the north side and octagonal piers on the south side are 13th century and so is the spacious chancel with pilaster buttresses and many lancets. The chancel south wall has sedilia with detached shafts and a piscina, a priest's doorway and five tall lancets. The chancel east window and several windows in the aisles plus the clerestory are early 16th century. The north aisle west window looks 14th century and the south aisle west window seems to go with the tower, which is 15th century and has bold corner buttresses and a SE corner stair turret. Two windows and the south porch and the NE vestry are Victorian. The porch protects a Norman doorway with scalloped capitals and a later arch. The vestry east doorway is 16th century work reset.

The initials W.W. on the stalls date them to between 1418-1434. They were made for the adjacent abbey church and have shafts and canopies. The misericords show on the south side a dragon, a man shoeing a goose, wine and grapes, a green man, an angel, Alexander carried to the sky by eagles, a pelican, pomegranates, and a lion and dragon, whilst on the north are Reynard the fox and a goose, St George and the dragon, two eagles feeding, a girl and a satyr, a plant, a rose, the signum triciput, a pig feeding on acorns, and a husband being beaten with a frying pan by his wife. There are late medieval screens under the chancel arch and dividing off chapels at the east end of each aisle. One pew has what may be the panels from the dado of an old screen. A pew called St Anton's Cage has inscriptions and dates of 1534, 1610 and 1830. The upper parts are of 1697. The next pew to the north has fine carving of 1702. At the west end are the churchwardens' pew dated 1690 and the constable's pew of 1714. There are benches with curly tops, one dated 1638. The organ case of 1729 has come from Lancaster. There is an octagonal 15th century font and there is an 18th century brass three-tier chandelier. The oldest of the monuments are the brasses to Ralph Caterall, d1515, shown kneeling with his wife and children, and the tablet by Fisher to Elizabeth Whalley, d1785. Outside are three Anglo-Saxon crosses, one of them having scrolls on the shaft. See p12 and inside front cover.

Whalley Church

WHITTINGTON   *St Michael*   SD 600763

The church has a commanding position on a ridge. In 1875 Colonel D.C.Greene had most of it rebuilt, especially the east end. Original late medieval work are the western four bays of each arcade, the west tower with diagonal buttresses with many offsets and a NE stair turret, and some of the outer walling on the north and south sides. The aisles are quite narrow, although they widen very slightly to form chapels flanking the chancel.

WHITTLE-LE-WOODS   *St Chad*   *SD 578215*

The three bay long transepts with arcade piers on granite columns formed part of the church of 1791. The rest is of 1896 and Italianate in style with arched windows and a west tower with a low pyramidal roof.

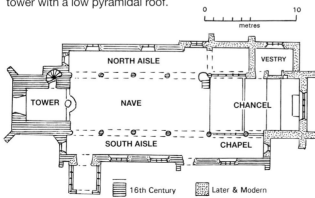

Plan of Whittington Church

Whittington Church

Winwick Church   *St George's Church, Wigan*

WIGAN   *All Saints*   SD 581058

Much of the church dates from the rebuilding of 1845-50 by Sharpe and Paley, although they are said to have reproduced what was already there. Genuine old parts are the 13th century lower stage of the tower, with a west window of stepped lancets, much of the nave roof, and the north chapel as rebuilt c1620, although the two bay arcade between it and the chancel may be 15th century work. The nave and aisle have arcades of six bays of late medieval type and there are two rood-stair turrets. A Roman altar is built into the walling of the church. The tapestry dorsal showing the Death of Ananias is a rare survival from the period of Archbishop Laud. Very mutilated effigies survive of what are thought to be Sir William de Bradshaigh and his wife who founded a chantry in the church in 1338. Only the head remains of the effigy of a medieval priest. Later monuments include those of James Bankes, d1689, and John Baldwin, d1726. During a Parliamentary attack upon Wigan in 1643 the top of the church tower was manned by Royalist sharpshooters.

WIGAN   *St George*   SD 584059

A baluster type font of c1710 from All Saints lies in the brick church of 1781 with four bays of arched windows in two tiers. The doorway has a broken pediment on columns and a shaped gable. Two giant columns divide off a short chancel inside.

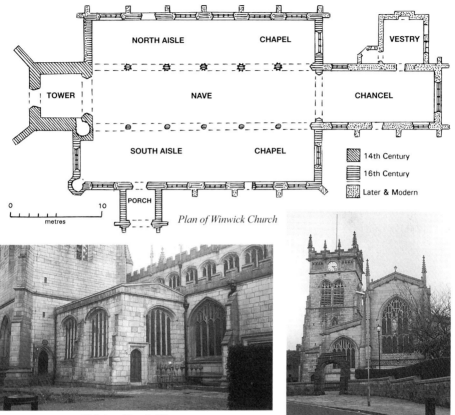

Plan of Winwick Church

14th Century
16th Century
Later & Modern

All Saints Church, Wigan

All Saints Church, Wigan

WINWICK   *St Oswald*   SJ 604927

The 14th century west tower has niches on either side of the west window. Other old parts are the north aisle east wall and the west wall and SW turret of the south aisle. On the aisle west wall is the date 1530 and an inscription recording the "renovatio" of the wall by the priest Henry Johnson and commemorating King Oswald of Northumbria, killed in 642, supposedly on this site. The piers of the north arcade are far two big for the arches they support. Probably there has been rebuilding here c1600 reusing older material. The chancel and vestry are of 18347-8 by Pugin. The clerestory is 16th century. The Victorian aisle windows with plaques with IHS in the intersections of mullions and transoms probably reproduce work of the 1530s. In the Gerard chapel on the north side is a fragment of a large late medieval font and the cross-bar of the head of a huge Anglo Saxon cross carved with interlace, humans and animals. Only loose fragments remain of the medieval rood loft. A small panel of uncertain date at the west end is carved with a pig. The brass chandelier is probably 18th century. In the Gerard chapel is a worn brass of Piers Gerard, d1495, under a triple canopy. On the Legh chapel on the south side is a brass depicting Sir Peter Legh, d1527 and his wife. He was ordained after her death and wears priestly vestments under his armour. The many other monuments include that of eight year old Benet Legh, d1755, and one to Richard Legh, d1687 with freestanding busts.

WOOD PLUMPTON   *St Anne*   SD 499344

Fragments of a Norman church here were found during the restoration of 1900 when the roof was provided with dormer windows. The arcades are late medieval and so is the north aisle if it is accepted that the window of c1300 with a rounded trefoil over pointed-trefoiled lights is reset. The tower with an octagonal cupola and the south aisle are of 1748. The aisle is embattled with arched windows with key stones and doorways with Baroque surrounds in the first and fifth bays from the west.

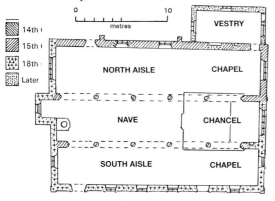

Plan of Wood Plumpton Church

Brass at Winwick

Wood Plumpton Church

OTHER LANCASHIRE CHURCHES EXISTING BEFORE 1800

AINSWORTH - Christchurch - 1831-2 on site of 16th century chapel.
ANCOATS - St George - 1877 on site of late 18th century church.
ANCOATS - St Paul - 1876, replacing nearby church on 1765 in Turner Street.
ASHWORTH - St James - Nave 1789. 16th century chancel replaced in 1837.
ASTLEY - St Stephen - Brick church of 1760 demolished a few years after fire of 1961.
BOLTON - All Saints - 1869-71, now deconsecrated. On site of church of 1726-43.
BORWICK - A medieval chapel once stood upon the green.
CHORTON GREEN - Churchyard only of former church of 1779, demolished in 1949.
ECCLESTON - St Anne - Nave possibly of 1723, tower base 1841, rest all of 1884.
HAMBLETON - St Mary - Rebuilt in 18th cent. Looks early 19th, but tower dated 1877.
LITTLE LEVER - Paley's church of 1865 replaced a church of 1791.
LIVERPOOL - Robson's church of 1870 replaced one of 1770 with cast-iron galleries.
MILNROW - St James - 1868 by Street. Medieval church here rebuilt in 1798 and 1815.
MORECAMBE - Holy Trinity - Edward Sharpe's church of 1840 replaced one of 1745.
MOSSLEY - St George - 1879-82, tower added 1887. On site of church of 1755-7.
NEWCHURCH - St Nicholas - The original parish church of Rawtenstall founded c1511
    and rebuilt c1560. Present church is of 1825-6, chancel added, etc, 1898.
NEWTON HEATH - All Saints - 1814,1844 & 1880. Church existed here in 1573.
OLDHAM - St Margaret - 1880, tower 1906. On site of church of 1766-9.
OLDHAM - St Mary - 1823-7 by Richard Lane. A church was recorded here in 1448.
PRESTON - St George - 1845 & 1884 on site of chapel-of-ease of 1723.
RAINFORD - All Saints - 1878, tower 1903. Near to site of church erected in 1577.
ROYTON - St Paul - Cockburn's church of 1884-9 lies on site of a church of 1754.
RUSHOLME - St James - 1845-6 by J.M.Derick on site of chapel built in 1595.
SHAW - Holy Trinity - 1870. Church standing here in 1515 was rebuilt in 1739 & 1800.
SWINTON - St Peter - 1869 by G.E.Street, replacing a large plain chapel of 1791.
WEST DERBY - St Mary - 1853 by G.G.Scott. Replaced 1793 church on medieval site.
WESTHOUGHTON - St Bartholomew - 1869. Medieval church here was rebuilt in 1731.
WHITECHAPEL - St James - Built in 1738 but now essentially of 1818 and 1889.

OTHER CHURCHES CONTAINING ANCIENT FURNISHINGS

FRECKLETON - Holy Trinity - 1837. Pulpit of 1633 with arabesques from Kirkham.
HARWOOD - Christchurch - 1840. Altar-table of 1561 from Nuremberg. Late 17th
    century pulpit from St James' Palace, London. Flemish Baroque eagle lecturn.
    Stalls with miserichords carved with faces and foliage.
KNOWSLEY - St Mary - Flemish 16th & 18th century stalls from Hall in church of 1843.
PARBOLD - Christchurch - 1875 - Pulpit of 1648 from Douglas chapel down by the river.
WORSLEY - 1846 by G.G.Scott. Pulpit and organ screen contain 16th and 17th century
    carved panels from Northern England, Flanders and France.

FURTHER READING

Victoria County Histories of Lancashire (Several volumes, various dates)
North Lancashire, Nicholas Pevsner, Buildings of England series, 1969
South Lancashire, Nicholas Pevsner, Buildings of England series, 1969
Lancashire & Cheshire Antiquarian Society annual proceedings.

A GLOSSARY OF TERMS

Apse   - Semicircular or polygonal east end of a church contain an altar.
Architrave - The lowest of the three main parts of the entablature of an order.
Ashlar - Masonry of blocks with even faces and square edges.
Baroque - A whimsical and odd form of the Classical architectural style.
Broaches - Sloping half-pyramids adapting an octagonal spire to a square tower.
Cartouche - A tablet with an ornate fram, usually enclosing an inscription.
Chancel - The eastern part of a church used by the clergy.
Clerestory - An upper storey pierced by windows lighting the floor below.
Crossing Tower - A tower built upon four arches in the middle of a cruciform church.
Cruciform Church - A cross-shaped church with transepts forming the arms of the cross.
Cusp - A projecting point between the foils of a foiled Gothic arch.
Dado - The decorative lower part of a wall or screen.
Decorated - The archtectural style in vogue in England c1300 - 1380
Elizabethan - Of the time of Queen Elizabeth I (1558 - 1603).
Fan Vault - Vault with fan-like patterns. In fashion from c1440 to 1530.
Fleche - Slender spire usually of wood set on the central part of a roof.
Foil - A lobe formed by the cusping of a circle or an arch.
Four-centred Arch - A low, flattish arch with each curve drawn from two compass points.
Hammer-beam Roof - Roof carried on arched braces set on beams projecting from a wall.
Head-stops - Heads of humans or beasts forming the ends of a hoodmould.
Hoodmould - A projecting moulding above a lintel or arch to throw off water.
Jacobean - Of the time of King James I (1603-25).
Jamb - The side of a doorway, window, or other opening.
Lancet - A long and comparatively narrow window usually with a pointed head.
Light - A compartment of a window.
Lintel - A horizontal stone or beam spanning an opening.
Low-side Window - A window with a low sill allowing those outside a chancel to see inside.
Miserichord - A bracket underneath hinged choir stall seat to support standing person.
Mullion - A vertical member dividing the lights of a window.
Nave - The part of a church in which the congregation sits or stands.
Norman - A division of English Romanesque architecture from 1066 to c1200.
Ogival Arch - Arch of oriental origin with both convex and concave curves.
Pediment - Low-pitched gable over an end wall or a doorway or window.
Perpendicular - The architectural style in vogue in England c1380 - 1540.
Pilaster - Flat buttress or pier attached to a wall.
Piscina - A stone basin used for rinsing out holy vessels after a mass.
Plinth - The projecting base of a wall.
Quoin - A dressed stone at the corner of a building.
Rebus - A visual pun or play on words, usually referring to someone's surname.
Rere-Arch - An inner arch such as the internal arch over a window or doorway opening.
Respond - A half pier or column bonded into a wall and carrying an arch.
Rood Screen - A screen with a crucifix mounted on it between a nave and a chancel.
Sedilia - Seats for clergy (usually three) in the south wall of a chancel.
Spandrel - The surface beween two arches, or between an arch and a wall.
Tester - A sounding-board above a 17th or 18th century pulpit.
Tie-Beam - A beam connecting the slopes of a roof at or near its foot.
Tracery - Intersecting ribwork in the uppe parts of a later Gothic window.
Transom - A horfizontal member dividing the lights of a window.
Tuscan - An order of Classical Architecture.
Tympanum - The space between the lintel of a doorway and the arch above it.
Venetian Window - Window with a square-headed light on either side of an arched light.
Victorian - Of the time of Queen Victoria (1837- 1901).
Wind-Braces - Struts used to strengthen the sloping sides of a gabled roof.